Out of the Canyon

Art & Allison Daily

Out of the Canyon

A True Story of Loss and Love

Harmony Books
NEW YORK

Published in the United States by Harmony Books, an imprint of the
Crown Publishing Group, a division of Random House, Inc., New York.
www.crownpublishing.com

Harmony Books is a registered trademark and the Harmony Books
colophon is a trademark of Random House, Inc.

Grateful acknowledgment is made to Nancy Wood for permission
to reprint the poem "Of Mountains and Women," from *Spirit Walker*
by Nancy Wood, copyright © 1993 by Nancy Wood. Reprinted
by.permission of the author.

Library of Congress Cataloging-in-Publication Data
Daily, Art.
    Out of the canyon / Art Daily and Allison Daily.—1st ed.
        p. cm.
    1. Daily, Art. 2. Grief—Case studies. 3. Bereavement—
Psychological aspects—Case studies. 4. Death—Psychological
aspects. 5. Loss (Psychology) I. Daily, Allison. II. Title.
    BF575.G7D35 2009
    155.9'370922—dc22   2008050583

ISBN 978-0-307-40940-9

Printed in the United States of America

Design by Lynne Amft

10 9 8 7 6 5 4 3 2 1

First Edition

Nothing worth doing is completed in our lifetime; therefore, we must be saved by hope. Nothing true or beautiful or good makes complete sense in any immediate context of history; therefore, we must be saved by faith. Nothing we do, however virtuous, can be accomplished alone; therefore, we are saved by love.

—REINHOLD NIEBUHR

Contents

Authors' Note

*O**ut of the Canyon* represents our joint effort to explore what happens when people experience great loss but still find the power to live and love again. Because we are two such people, and each of us has a unique perspective on the events that unfolded, we have written the story in our alternating voices. You will see two different typefaces—one for Art and one for Allison.

We know that your story is different from ours, probably in countless ways. Yet in deep grief there are universal elements that touch us all and that bring forth the shimmering truths of who we really are—our fierceness, our compassion, the essential grace and beauty of which we are made. We hope that our story will help you to find these things in your own experience and that it may bring you solace and hope and the inspiration to move forward, whatever losses you may have suffered.

As in any memoir, the dialogue recorded here is reconstructed to the best of our ability. It is as accurate a reflection of the conversations that took place as we can make it. The names of friends and loved ones have not been changed, with the gracious consent of those who are still living.

Some of our early readers asked for something beyond the story itself—for something more about how we connect with one another during the grieving process. So we have added an epilogue of sorts, "Upon Reflection," in which you will find further observations on what helped each of us— and sometimes what didn't—as we dealt with the tragedies in our lives.

Art and Allison Daily

Foreword

by Pam Houston

Strangers often write to me. One day I received an e-mail
from Allison Daily. It was much too long and way too personal to be a typical fan letter. Its contents described events
all over the world, from Colorado's Glenwood Canyon to
Anguilla Island in the Lesser Antilles, from Austin to Aspen,
from Independence Pass to the Grand Canyon's Tanner Trail.
Allison went into a lot of detail about herself, her marriage to
Art, her brother's suicide, and a terrible accident of a decade
ago (I had a vague memory of hearing about it at the time)
that happened on Highway 70 in which a man lost his whole
family when a boulder fell from high on the canyon wall and
crushed the car he was driving, leaving him inexplicably untouched. The letter neither flinched nor apologized as it made
giant leaps between what I've always (with some reservations)
called the "real" world to other planes of existence, to dimen-
sions beyond what we can know.

I get a lot of e-mail from crazy people. It comes with the
territory of being a writer and a public figure. There are

complete strangers who want to marry me, who want to sue me, who want to perform an exorcism on me at the W Hotel. To this day I don't know what kept me from hitting the delete button after I read Allison's letter. Allison assumed, rightly as it turned out, that I was the sort of person who had always suspected angels were out there, who had watched *Wings of Desire* a hundred times with nothing in my heart but hope and longing, but who still hadn't ever dared make the leap into belief.

"You're going all the way to Aspen to meet this person?" my friend Practical Karen asked me.

"Not really," I said. "I'm driving from Steamboat Springs to Creede next Friday. Aspen is more or less on the way."

"Don't come crying to me," Practical Karen said, "when she wants you to have her baby."

"I have a feeling about this one," I said to Karen, and every once in a blue moon, my feelings are actually right.

I knew it the moment I walked into Matsuhisa and saw their blond heads bent together over the sushi menu at the bar. Allison and Art leaped out of their chairs when they saw me, we shook hands, then hugged, then shook hands again, all three of us grinning ear to ear like idiots. (I found out later that they hate sushi, but they had asked me what my favorite restaurant in Aspen was, and that night they slurped a lot of very expensive fish down their throats for me.) It wasn't only that they glowed—and they did glow, both of them, with health and life and love for the world and each other—but it was as if the three of us had been reunited after a long and unhappy separation, and now that we were in proximity, the world had righted itself again.

That night they started telling me the incredible story that now fills these pages. They asked me to help them. I said, without hesitation, without really understanding how I *might* help them, that I would.

Over the course of the next two years we discovered, together, that helping meant showing Allison how she could channel all her enthusiasm and no-holds-barred emotion into concrete physical description that would be accessible to a reader, how to take her revelations and turn them into scenes. Art was already a fine lawyer and a fine writer, so helping him meant giving him the courage to access a little less of the lawyer on the page, and a little more of the human being. After that it was a matter of reading drafts, of trying to get them excited about revision, of making suggestions for exclusion or inclusion, of saying yes when they asked me if the story was worth telling, and yes when they wondered if anyone would believe them, and yes when they said that they guessed it wouldn't matter, because by that time the writing had become its own reward.

I could tell you that what I've gotten in return for my commitment to *Out of the Canyon* is a lot of great days of skiing and hiking, a handful of great dinners at the Woody Creek Tavern (no more sushi!), a full scholarship for a young writer to attend a conference I run in California, and some really great earrings, and all of those things would be true. I could tell you that I've gotten a be-there-for-you-in-the-middle-of-any-given-night kind of friend in Allison and a make-you-glad-you-are-on-the-same-planet-with-this-man kind of friendship with Art, that in the last two years Allison and Art and their beautiful boys, Rider and Burke, have become four of the most important people in the world to me, and that, too, would be true. I could tell you that there is a woman named Kathy, who used to be married to Art, who died with their sons, Tanner and Shea, on the day a boulder fell from the top of Glenwood Canyon, but who now looks out—in her very complicated, tough-love way—for Art and Allison and their two boys, and *even* sometimes for me, and you don't yet have any reason to believe me, but with a gun to my head I would swear it is true. But what I am is a writer and a teacher of writing, so what I really want to tell you is that I read *Out of the Canyon* five times, in five different manuscript stages—more than that if you count the early days when it was in fragments—and I was moved, as if for the first time, every single time. I never lost my attention for the story. I felt that with each reading I was taking something more and different and deeper away from it. What I really want to tell you is that the pleasure has been all mine.

Several years ago I traveled extensively in the country of Bolivia. On the long dirt road that climbs out of the lush Yungas Valley, up and over the Cordillera Real and down onto the dry Altiplano, dogs stand sentinel like toll takers hoping for scraps of bread and chicken. There is also a man who stands there, a human stoplight, my guide Marcelo called him, who lost his entire family in a crash on the blind corner where we found him standing one hot afternoon, holding a small red flag in the air.

"He has been there every day for the three years since the crash," Marcelo said, "and he says he will stand there for the rest of his life."

Our driver, Ramone, slowed the 4Runner to a stop in front of him. We watched him look in both directions, lower the red flag, then raise the green. Ramone rolled down the window to give him some tired *grenadillas* from the backseat and a half a loaf of bread. He saluted the vehicle, and we went on our way.

"Some people think he is crazy," Marcelo said, "and other people think this thing he does is very good. But everyone who passes gives him something. Everyone says, 'It could have been any one of us.' "

It *could* have been any one of us, but it *was* Art Daily. A man who lost everything to a rock in Glenwood Canyon. A man who experienced grief so complete that it almost killed him. A man who took a great deal of time and painstaking care to emerge from that grief whole and glowing, dedicated to helping others through the caverns of cataclysmic loss, and nudging the rest of us toward a greater appreciation of what hasn't been taken away.

The book you hold in your hand is a man standing on the road in Bolivia with a red and a green flag in his hand. It is a testimony to the fact that though the missing never ends, the jaws of grief one day finally loosen. It is proof that honest emotion always wins in the end, even when it is difficult and painful and complicated. It is a prayer of thanks to the ones we have lost and the power, the love that allows them to stay with us. It is a book whose pages are filled with the purest kind of light.

Some people will think that Art and Allison are crazy. I might have been one of them, but as it turned out, I was not. Some powerful force brought Allison and Art together, and some version of that same force brought me into their lives. You might call it coincidence; another person might call it serendipity. We happen to call her Kathy. Once you've read their story, you can call her anything you like.

Out of the Canyon

Where Dreams End

THE BOULDER HAS RESTED HIGH UP ON THE CANYON WALLS
for a thousand years or more. Now it has broken loose and is
hurtling down toward the westbound lanes of Interstate 70
in Glenwood Canyon, one of the most spectacular stretches of
roadway in our country. The rugged cliffs reach far into the sky
on either side of us, carved through the millennia by the Colorado River, which winds along the floor of the canyon. The
highway is an engineering wonder to all who travel it. I have
come this way more times than I can count, and now Kathy,
my wife of twelve years, and our sons, Tanner and Shea, are
returning to our home in Aspen from a youth hockey game in
Vail.

The peacefulness of the drive is suddenly shattered. I
catch a fleeting glimpse of the beast as it hits the ground next
to the Suburban and then smashes into the passenger side
where Kathy is dreaming. The great rock continues on its path
over the top of the vehicle, tearing at the roof with a grinding
shriek that will always be with me. It is like being broadsided

by a train. The force and the sound of the impact are terrifying, and the big car is slammed halfway into the other lane. I stand on the brake pedal and fight the steering wheel back under control, finally bringing us to a spark-flying stop along the right hand guard rail. A profound silence settles upon the car.

Beyond reason, I am untouched. I look across the front seat at Kathy. The left side of her head is unmarked, but I know that she is dead. The door and window where she is sitting are exploded inward, and she cannot have survived. A chunk of flesh is lying between my feet. It must be part of her. She looks strangely peaceful. I reach across and touch her hair. "Kathy," I choke out. "Oh, Kathy."

Ripping off my seat belt, I look back at our boys. We'd lowered the middle seats, and Tanner and Shea have been buckled into their third-row seats watching a movie on the portable VCR. Nothing will ever compare with the horror of that moment. The middle section of the vehicle is mangled, and I can see the late afternoon sky through a hole in the roof. The boys are lying on the seat beneath the flattened roof, and neither is moving or making a sound. My soul cracks wide open, and as I crawl and fight my way back between the seats I scream and scream at the sky. A man is running up the highway toward us, and he slows for a moment as he hears me. By now I am on my knees next to the boys trying to lift the twisted metal off them, and the man climbs onto the car and reaches in through the tear in the roof to help. Finally we free them and I lift first Tanner and then Shea up to the man, who

gently places them side by side on the edge of the highway. I
will never know his name.

Inexplicably, they do not look badly wounded, although
there is evidence of a deep trauma on the right side of Tanner's forehead. Shea just appears to be sleeping. Somehow,
though, I know in my heart that they are both desperately hurt
and that I may lose them. Oh dear God, these are beautiful
boys, and I love them with all my soul. On my knees I move
from one to the other trying to breathe life into them, to keep
them alive. I've descended into madness. I alternate between
praying to God over and over to save my sons, desperate grieving, and screaming in blind rage at the rocks towering above
me toward the clouds. I know that help will be on the way, but
we are on an elevated highway in the middle of sixteen miles
of canyon, there are few exits, and I learn later that the ambulances from Glenwood Springs have to go all the way to the
top of the canyon before they can circle back down the westbound lanes.

Two doctors from Oregon get out of their car and hurry
over to see if they can help. They pull breathing tubes and
stethoscopes out of their medical bags and listen for signs of
life while taking over the artificial breathing from me. Tanner
has a faint heartbeat, but they can detect nothing in Shea. I
kneel helplessly next to the boys, talking to them, telling them
over and over how much I love them, my whole essence con-
centrated on transferring my power, my strength, my aliveness
into my dying sons. I'm scared it will take a vital force greater
than mine to change their fate. I am so hopelessly alone.

I ask one of the doctors if he will check on Kathy. He stands up from the roadside and moves quickly over to the Suburban. He reaches in through the shattered window for a minute or two, and then walks back toward me, sorrow etched across his face, shaking his head gently from side to side. He returns to working with the boys.

A man leaves his wife and children in their car and comes to stand beside me on the roadway. His son played with Shea on the Aspen Mites hockey team in the game that we are all returning home from, and he had introduced himself to me in a pizza place after the game. Cecil is a quiet and reserved man, yet his presence is deeply comforting. "Can I help in any way?" he asks. "I don't know," I say. "They're not doing very well." He stays with me in my anguish. He hears me begging to God to help them breathe, to make them conscious once again. "Dear Lord," I cry, "if they cannot both survive, please save one of them." In some way Cecil is cradling me with his spirit. Who is this stranger who cares enough to be with me in this bleakness, this horror? I still wonder at his courage.

Two ambulances finally weave their way through the slow-moving traffic, mournful sirens echoing in the ancient canyon. Nurses and EMTs jump out and check on Tanner and Shea, and one of them also looks in on Kathy, but there is nothing to be done for her. They speak briefly with the Oregon doctors, who are still by the boys' side, quickly lift Shea into the first ambulance and speed off down the highway toward Valley View Hospital in Glenwood Springs. They suggest that I ride with Tanner in the second ambulance. It is clear to me that they think Shea is in the more critical condition, that Tanner has the better chance to survive. I help carry Tanner's gurney to the back of the ambulance, and then I climb into the front seat next to the driver.

The drive down out of the canyon seems endless, though it probably takes no more than twenty minutes, and I can hear the nurse speaking anxiously with the doctors at the hospital. I keep talking to Tanner down the little hallway that separates the front seats from the caregiving part of the ambulance. "Stay with us, Tanner, please try to stay with me. I love you so very much. We're almost there." Tanner, I believe, is fighting to come back to his father.

We pull into the emergency entrance to the hospital, and an EMT hurries out to hold the door open for Tanner's gurney. He doesn't quite meet my eye, and my fear for Shea stabs deeper. I'm led into a waiting area, and I'm aware of frenzied activity in two emergency rooms near me. I feel as if I've passed into some barren and savage zone, between knowing and unknowing, where the extreme dread and desperation have given way to liminal space, a time between things. I am waiting for God.

As I sit there, Cecil and his wife, Noelle, arrive to be with me. Someone approaches and suggests that I might be more comfortable in the small hospital chapel next to the waiting room, then leads me to it. Cecil and Noelle come with me. I stand numbly before a little altar with a wooden cross on it, running my hands over the cross while looking blindly at a colorful stained-glass window in the wall. I clasp my hands together, crying and praying helplessly. I don't know what else to do. A doctor enters the chapel and stands by the door. He looks at me, then quietly tells me, "I'm sorry, we couldn't save either one."

I scream and fall to the floor, curling up like a child. They're all gone. All I want is to be with them. I don't want to go on without them. There are no words to describe where I have gone, what I am beginning to see. Noelle and Cecil try to hold me, to give what comfort they can. Eventually I climb back to my feet and we walk out of the chapel into the emergency area. I ask to be with my children.

A nurse leads me first to one room and says, "One of your sons is here," and then leads me to the adjoining room and says, "The other is here." In each room a naked child lies peacefully on his back on a gurney. Their eyes are closed. There is an eternal stillness about them. They are no longer here. But I am. What can I do? I go from one room to the other and then back again. Why can't they be together, when they were so incredibly close in life? I want to pick up one son and carry him to be with the other. I wish that Kathy's body was here with us, too, in these last moments, but with her awful head injuries I think she might not have wanted that.

The starkness of this final place is surreal. How do I tell my children what I am feeling, what I have always felt, what I will feel through eternity? I do what I can. I touch their faces, their eyes, their lips. I tell each of them, many times, how much I love them, that I will always love them, that somehow we will always be together. I ask their forgiveness for the things that I was not, as a man and a father. I ask God to receive them in great love and beauty, to take away their wounds and their pain, to embrace them in eternal joy and happiness. I beseech God to keep our love alive beyond this death, to bind our hearts and souls forever as one. Then I say good-bye to them, one at a time, and I turn away and leave them.

In the waiting area a priest is sitting by himself, hoping to talk with me. He doesn't know my faith, and I don't learn his, but he has come to be with me. He is a kind man who knows human anguish, and we spend a few quiet minutes together. A nurse approaches and asks softly if I would be willing to allow Tanner and Shea's vital organs to be used to help other children. The boys answer through me, "Of course." I am becoming aware that life around me continues to move on, that only mine has stopped. How am I ever going to be part of it again?

There is a call that I must make. Piper, my beloved daughter from my first marriage, also lives in Aspen, and she doesn't know yet about Kathy and her brothers. She is twenty-four now, a good deal older than Tanner (who would have been eleven next month) and Shea (who is six), but they love each other very much. When she picks up the phone I tell her, in a voice that she can hardly hear, "Piper, I have some terrible news . . ." As soon as she hears it, she bursts into tears, and cries, "Oh Dad, I can't believe it. Are you all right? I love you so much. I'll meet you at the house."

Cecil and Noelle are patiently waiting for me. God bless them. There is no one else. Noelle has arranged to ride home with another hockey family, and Cecil asks, "Art, where do you want me to take you?" I can already feel the deep emptiness of my house, but I tell him, "I guess I want to go home." As we drive through the darkness toward Aspen, about an hour away, I hug my knees in desperation, rocking back and forth, and I cry out to Cecil, "Where am I going to put my love?" Side by side we sit, crying. Time and again he reaches over to touch me. He understands there are no words. The road seems to stretch away to nowhere.

When There Is No Light

IT'S A DARK FEBRUARY NIGHT IN A QUIET NEIGHBORHOOD. We drop down the driveway of our home at the base of Red Butte. There's a low light on in the living room. Several cars are parked along the driveway, and I can see that word of the accident has preceded us and that the first close friends have come to be with me. Cecil is concerned about leaving me and offers to come in and stay for a while. I turn to him and tell him that I won't be alone, that he needs to rejoin his own family. They will be wondering and worrying about him. I try to find words, any words, to express my feelings about the love and compassion and grace that he has given to me this day. He raises a hand to quiet me and folds me once again in his embrace. He says, "Art, if you need me, just call." I get out of the car and walk to the house, always so alive with the shouts and laughter of Kathy, Shea, and Tanner, now silent and empty. It feels as though the entire fabric and composition of my world are gone. Who am I now? The trackless darkness is deepening around me, without bottom or end.

Good people meet me at the door. Deborah, Aspen Mountain ski patroller and medicine woman, leader of vision quests. Jim, my law partner whose own four-year-old son died in his sleep several years ago. Boots, another partner, Bob Dylan in his soul. Tommy, a sweet and pure friend who builds fine homes. The kind of people who always seem to show up when the going is the hardest. Each of them holds me close, without words. They must be wondering, "What can we do for this man; how do we keep him alive?" We sit close to one another and talk a little, and I tell them what I can of my experience. They, too, are desolate. A wife and mother and her sons are gone. What purpose can possibly have been served by this? We don't speak of the future, of any time beyond this evening, this moment.

They know that Piper will be arriving soon, and Boots leads me into another room and asks if I want to change my pants and shirt before she gets here. I look down and am surprised by the blood on my clothes. From the boys, I guess, although I don't seem to remember much bleeding. I go upstairs to change, hearing for the first time the awful stillness and loneliness of empty rooms. As I return to the kitchen, Tommy quietly inquires if I own any guns. "I do," I respond, "I've got an old long-barrel Ruger pistol, with holster and gun belt, on the top shelf of a closet. It's got a key lock on the trigger guard." He says he'd like to take care of it for me for a while, so I track it down and pass it over to him in the garage. A thoughtful thing to do. I haven't been thinking about dying, but every fiber of my being is crying out to be with my family.

Piper drives up and comes running into the house. "Dad," she says. "Oh Dad, are you okay?" And she puts her arms around me and holds me to her fierce and gentle spirit. Deborah and Piper replace the lamplight with candles, and the six of us stand and hold one another in a close circle for a long time, moving silently along our outstretched arms. Deborah calls upon ancient spirits for courage and faith and other things that we need tonight. For reasons she cannot explain, Piper reaches into her pocket and finds an angel card for healing. A little dazed, she shows it to us and asks if anyone put it there. As I now look out and back, I see that this was but the first of many wonders, both great and small, that have since filled my life with a sweetness and a ferocity that I would not have believed possible. But on this first night I cannot know any of these things, and tomorrow is far, far away.

One by one my friends reluctantly leave, and Piper and I are alone. Someone has kindly left me a sleeping pill, and I bite off half and swallow it down. We move upstairs to Kathy's and my bedroom, and Piper drags a large sleeper cushion in from the boys' playroom and sets up a sleeping area for herself at the foot of my bed. We turn off the lights and talk and then try to get some sleep. Before long I get out of bed and walk back downstairs. Piper follows me down. She finds me sitting on the floor in the middle of the darkened living room, arms tightly around my knees, rocking back and forth and crying uncontrollably. She sits on the rug nearby and keeps me company. Hours go by before we finally return to bed and fall asleep. Grief. What an awesomely dark and terrible place.

I've read and heard of so many tragedies, affecting individual people and families and entire tribes, but the loss of a child assaults the human spirit in ways that can be neither imagined nor described. I am so helplessly alone, so altogether without hope.

Waking to Forever

PALE WINTER LIGHT FILTERS THROUGH THE WINDOWS. AS I return to consciousness, without warning the realization of what has happened shatters me. There are no sounds, no words. My whole being suddenly knows that all mornings will bring the same stark and terrible truth: Kathy and the boys are gone, they will not be with me today—or ever again. How can I go on, comprehending this? I am so heavy. What do I do if I get out of bed? How do I walk in the daylight, when I am filled with darkness? Will I ever sleep again, knowing that I will only awaken to this same nightmare? I have come to a place from which I cannot return, and I do not know how to be here.

I close my eyes again and Kathy comes to me. I can almost see her—long blonde hair dropping over her shoulders, fierce strength shining in her deep brown eyes. Kathy was a powerful spirit and a loner in many ways, and I sometimes wondered that she bothered to marry me in the first place. She maintained her clear course in life despite my occasional wildness and selfishness, and she continually challenged me when I strayed too far from being a thoughtful and helpful person. What began as a love affair had evolved into more of a partnership and, in the last year or so, into a deepening friendship. Kathy was a fine artist who could work in almost any medium. Her greatest love, I think, was portrait photography, and during the past several years she had been going out onto the far-flung farms and ranches in our valley to photograph the old-timers, many of whom were born here during the mining days, and to gather their stories. She told them she was going to write a book about them and their time, and as they came slowly to trust in her the word spread about the blonde woman and the two young boys whom she often brought with her, and more and more remote doors opened to her that had not seen a stranger for a long time. She photographed each man and each woman, and she let them choose which picture would appear in the book.

The title is *Aspen: The Quiet Years*, and it tells the story of the people who lived in the Roaring Fork Valley in the time between the end of the mining days around 1900 and the beginning of the skiing era after World War II. It's a beautiful book, and it was published several months before the accident. Kathy coauthored it with Gaylord Guenin, another local writer. Many mornings as I was heading off to work Kathy would sit me down at the breakfast table and have me edit the latest text before she sent it off to the real editor and eventually to the publisher. We had a lot of fun in the evenings, when she would show me her latest photographs and tell me stories of the people she had interviewed that day and of the lives they led. I realize now how much closer together the writing of that book brought us and how much more deeply I came to understand her artistic talents, her bawdy sense of humor, and her commitment to telling the true story.

Kathy, my girl, how am I going to do this? I ache with the missing of you, and I seem to ache even more with the missing of the boys. I know you understand. As their father I still want to protect them, even though they are gone. Fathers live in the very essence of their sons, and I long for mine with everything that I am. The morning light grows brighter, and I look over to where Kathy used to sleep next to me. I reach out and touch the empty place and I think of her own great love for Tanner and Shea. Part of me is thankful that she is with them, as I know that she would have wanted it this way. I send her my heart, and tears roll down my face.

When I finally sit up Piper softly greets me. "Good morning, Dad, let's go downstairs together." And so it begins. The rest of my life. Do I want to go on? Do I have the spirit, the courage, to do this? I don't know yet, but something moves me onward. Into the pain, the loneliness, the empty days. Even in this very early time, when I am in deepest shock, there is a raw spark, a glimmer of faith that is telling me that this is what we do. That we are indomitable beings. That we are made to persist, to stay the whole course—to find out who we are.

As I look back, the following days are indistinct, almost surreal. I am sheltered and comforted by family, friends, and acquaintances from near and far and sometimes by people I've never known. A lot of Kathy's buddies and many of my own—or those we shared—just walk in the door, man the phone and the kitchen, and tirelessly touch me and those around me with their love and affection. And the people of this small town where I have spent the better part of my adult life begin showing up, with flowers, and food, but mostly just to spend a few minutes with me, to hold me, to show me that they care. Together they fill the days and the early evenings, and they make all the difference. It is said that it takes a village to raise a child. Now I know that a community can keep a man afloat when his spirit is fragile and things hang in the balance. I don't really know how to describe what the love of this town meant to me, except to say that it meant that I still mattered, that I was not alone, that I would not have to do this by myself, that they would stay the course with me. And maybe above all, that they, too, loved Tanner and Shea and Kathy, in ways that touched and warmed me. The people of our town grieved this loss with me, and they have continued to do so down through the years.

John, one of my brothers, arrives from New York with his wife, Barbara, and their college-age children, Craig and Leigh. Along with Piper and another brother in Atlanta, they are the only close family I have left. Each in his or her own way gives me strength, but Barbara's compassion and wisdom are boundless.

From Denver comes a most extraordinary couple. Rob, a money manager, and his wife, Paula, a hair stylist, volunteer firefighter, and mother to four. But they are much more. They are healers; they change lives. Three or four times a year for the past ten years or so, they have led a weekend workshop in Aspen called Temenos, a Greek word for "sanctuary" or "safe place." It's a magical experience that has more than fifteen hundred graduates, and many of us just keep coming back to reopen ourselves and to help others move a few things around in their lives. Kathy cared deeply about people and believed in their ability to take charge of themselves. She was wholly committed to Temenos, and she took her tough love into the course room over and over again. It's a fragile and risky thing, telling people what they need to do to move on. Kathy got hurt a lot in that room, but she just kept on coming. There are a bunch of people around who are grateful that she took the chance for them, whose lives have been better since then. There's one in particular, a fine Aspen musician, who'd been bullshitting us for two days about his drinking. Kathy finally stood with him toe to toe and told him she loved him too much to stand by any longer and watch him kill himself. She said to him, "Bobby Mason, I can't be your friend anymore, not with the drinking." Shortly after, Bobby gave it up, and he's never looked back. He continues to tell folks, "Kathy Daily saved my life." She was that kind of girl. Man, I miss her.

Last night, and this first morning, and many mornings to come, I am blessed to have experienced Temenos. I'm conscious of my emotions, I can name them, and no matter how terrible the longing, how paralyzing the fear, at least I am not afraid of them. They won't kill me, though they may try. And now Paula and Rob are here again, helping me to go on, to take the first small steps. And Edgell has come, too, our preacher friend, the chaplain at Snowmass Chapel, a nondenominational church in nearby Snowmass Village. Edgell and Rob begin the unimaginable work of planning the memorial service for my family. They quickly bring together the people who wish to speak. Rob and Piper and Paula and Deborah. I would like Jim to say something—he's a caring and thoughtful man—but I'm concerned it may cause him to revisit too much of his own pain. When I ask him, though, he says, "Art, I'd be honored to say a few words." I don't understand until much later that this is what survivors of great loss do. We share what we know, what we've learned about ourselves, with others who must find a way to endure a crushing loss of their own. It's a payback for all the love that we've received, and maybe it brings some small meaning to what was otherwise such a senseless loss in our own lives.

I am upstairs in our bedroom, where Rob and Edgell have come to get away from people so they can work on the service, when a buddy of mine, a prominent lawyer in town and a member of the Jewish faith, stops in the doorway and asks if he can talk with me. He tells me that Joshua, a real estate broker who sometimes serves as a rabbi in their synagogue, would like to play a part in the service. Josh joins us, and explains that the Jewish community has been deeply affected by this tragedy and would like to participate in the healing. I think about it for a moment, and I realize that I am warmed by his offer. I have many Jewish friends, but this is a crossing over that seems to rise above our individual beliefs. I tell Josh that I would welcome his involvement, and he moves into the room to join the planners. I learn later that Josh quickly nixes the original choice of places as being too small and sets out himself to reserve Harris Hall, a beautiful new concert hall near the Aspen Music Festival Tent that holds more than five hundred people. To this day and even at the time, the role that Joshua played gave me an even greater sense of the community coming together to mourn our loss. It was a sensitive and gracious act, and it gave us all greater strength and purpose.

Edgell and Rob then come to me to ask if I want to say anything at the service. They tell me that it won't be expected of me, that it is really a matter of what I feel best about. I know the question has been in the back of my mind, but I haven't wanted to look at it. Do I have the words to tell our town about Kathy and Tanner and Shea, to describe who they really were, to say how much we loved each other? I don't think I do, but I know in my heart that I owe it to them, and to our friends—and maybe above all to myself—to try. I tell Rob that I will speak.

The service is set for Wednesday, two days from now. It is such an intense time, yet part of me feels detached, floating, in touch only with my inner voices, my raging feelings. I know now that Tanner and Kathy and Shea were with me all the time, each in their own way, holding me up, filling me with their love and their hope. They so much want me to understand that life does not end. As you will see, they have never left me, and they never will.

The house is filled with people from morning to dark. They all want to help in some way, if only by being there. They come from their offices, their homes, their schools. Each person finds a way to touch me, to say something, to hold me. Tanner and Shea's buddies flow in and out, stunned by this terrible accident. Most have never lost a friend before, and they are having trouble with the finality of it, with the deepening awareness that this isn't going to change, that Tanner and Shea won't be with them anymore. Their sadness and pain are so pure, they don't hide them. There are more of the older kids than the younger ones, and they all finally seek me out, sometimes with their parents and sometimes courageously alone. They say the best things like "I wish it hadn't happened," or "I'm really going to miss Tanner," or "Are you going to be all right?" Robbie Wade, from Tanner's hockey team, brings an eight-foot-long poster that he's painted and had signed by most of the fifth grade, and he takes me into the guest bedroom to spread it out and tell me about it. He's crying as he explains the pictures. So am I. I cry all the time, from sleep to sleep; no matter where I am or who I'm with, I just cry and cry. It's the flow of pain, on and on and on.

A young man I don't recognize has been standing inside the front door for a while now. He doesn't seem to know anyone. I walk over to be with him, and he tells me that he was Shea and Tanner's school bus driver and that he loved who they were and that his bus seems empty without them. He comes back to the house day after day, sitting by himself somewhere, so that he will not grieve alone, so that he can be a little closer to them.

Two of my own closest friends, Tony and Larry, take me for a walk around the block. One, the owner of commercial properties in Aspen, and the other one of the finest contemporary architects in the West. We've shared more than thirty years of intense experiences in these mountains, in the desert valleys to the west, and in other faraway places. We've let each other down from time to time, but the friendship has persisted. Now they walk on either side of me, as close as they can. I feel in the very marrow of me how much they care for me, how afraid they are for me, how much they want to help. If they could hold my hands, if they could cradle me in their arms and carry me between them, they would. But we have never done these things before, and we don't do them now. These men remain nearby for months to come, to be sure that I'm still on my feet, still moving forward. Sometimes it's good to have someone tall and strong to lean on.

In the midst of the craziness, the back of my mind is beginning to work on the things I want to say at the service. Tuesday evening, after most of our visitors have gone home, I sit down in Kathy's study to try to write something down. It quickly becomes apparent that I can't think very clearly here, so I climb into a car and drive down to my office. As I settle down at the computer and begin typing, I'm surprised by the flow of memories and feelings. I've never tried to put love and longing into words before, and the tears run down my face as I write. But the things that matter the very most to me become clear, and I continue to work into the night. I finally climb into bed about 4:30 a.m., the words that I have written stuffed under my pillow, and I lie there wondering how I'm going to get through this day. How do people do these things? Somehow I sleep.

Wednesday morning there is a blanket of new snow in

the valley, and a steady, silent snowfall continues through the day. Rain and snow have always brought me great peace, so I welcome the weather. There are some who say that if you can be present in perfect stillness in the snowfall and then open wide all your senses, you may witness angels darting and playing among the flakes. I don't have any trouble with that—I seem to be seeing my family in everything that moves. The snow does not work for everyone, though. I learn later that twenty-five partners in the Denver office of my law firm have chartered two planes to fly to Aspen to be here with me on this day, but the storm will not allow any landings in the mountains. They cannot drive here in time, and they are heartbroken.

Edgell brings an old friend of his to the house to meet me. Brad Ham is a burly, good-looking guy in his midforties, holding doctorates in both theology and psychology from prestigious institutions, and he's got this great boyish grin on his face. He's a clinical psychologist specializing in grief and loss, and I'm immediately attracted to him. We sit down in Kathy's study and he probes me with his mind and heart to see how I'm doing. Somehow I blurt out to this stranger how scared I am about everything, including things like the present and the future, how empty and lonely I feel, how little I seem to understand. Brad listens quietly, focused on me, and finally suggests that for now I just take things as they come, that I get through today. I tell him that I've tried to write down what I'm going to say, and for some reason I hand him a copy and ask him if he thinks it sounds appropriate. He reads it through and after looking at me for a few moments he says, "Thanks for letting me see this. You honor your wife and sons and your love for each other. I think it will be fine." I'm comforted by his comments, but I wonder why I wanted him to read it in the first place. I've just met the man, and here I am pouring out my soul and sharing my most intimate words. I guess I really wasn't feeling very confident or brave that day, and I needed to check in with someone. As it turns out, I chose a man who will play a pivotal role in guiding me through the darkness ahead.

When it is time, Rob and Paula and my family and I climb into a couple of airport vans for the drive over to Harris Hall. One of the vans is owned and driven by an old biker pal, and this ride to the service is his gift to me. It's incredible how people are—each gives what he or she can, always from the heart. As we walk into the hall I'm stunned by the number of people that have already arrived. They're standing in the back, in the aisles, and they continue to come until almost the entire stage area is covered with people sitting on the floor. I'm told later that hundreds could not get in at all, and waited patiently outside during the service. Aspen grieved that day. What a wonderful soul this town has. You could almost feel the spirits of the miners of the 1880s and their families, the people Kathy wrote so eloquently about in *Aspen: The Quiet Years.*

We take our seats near the front, behind an entire row of Aspen Squirts, the junior hockey team that Tanner played on, all wearing their jerseys. Piper is on one side of me, my brother John on the other. The service begins, and people speak lovingly, beautifully, and with great sorrow of Kathy, Tanner, and Shea, of all that we have lost. I feel numb and yet so alive, uplifted by the extraordinary compassion in the room, proud of today, afraid of all the days ahead. Eventually Edgell says, "Art, their husband and father, now wants to talk with you." I sit for a minute, caught between stillness and movement, and John asks softly, "Do you want me to come with you?" I tell him, "Thanks, I think I'll be all right," and I walk onto the stage to the lectern. I look out at the gathering of friends and acquaintances and strangers, waiting in silence. I begin to speak.

"I am so pleased that you are all here. I want you to know that what I am about to say is on behalf of Piper and myself.

"Along with Piper, Kathy and Tanner and Shea were my life. My joy. My dream. We loved each other so very much. And we were very proud of each other. We had so much fun together. I cherished them. And now, for reasons we'll never know, they've been taken from us. My heart is gone with them. It's hard to try to tell you anything about them that means anything at this time, because to me they were pure love, absolute light. But I still want to try.

"Kathleen Krieger Daily was one outrageous woman. She could make absolutely anything happen. Down at the old Public House, it was Halloween. I was dressed as an Arab prince. Kathy called her friend DeDe that night and said, 'Guess what, I'm going to marry a sheik.' She hadn't mentioned the plan to me, but you know the rest of the story.

"Kathy was an amazingly creative artist. Our house is filled with her paintings, her photographs, her scrimshaw. The most wonderful thing about Kathy was her profound caring for other people, her rare courage to try to improve people's lives. She touched so many people. *Touched* is probably too mild a word. It was more like being grabbed by the scruff of the neck and dragged along. She took huge risks with people, and sometimes she would really get hurt in the process. But she never quit sticking her neck out.

"There's no question that I was her greatest challenge. And she took immense pleasure in keeping me in line. But you know, in spite of all the kicking and screaming that I did, I owe her more than I could ever describe. She helped me to believe in myself in so many ways. The strength that Kathy gave me has helped me to be here with you today. She was also funny, and she was totally irreverent. I remember at the ripe age of forty-nine I spent weeks trying to learn how to windsurf at Kanaha on Maui. I'd come home all beat up. Kathy loved it, and started calling me 'Moon Doggie.' And ever since then, whenever she was particularly amused by me, she'd talk about Moon Doggie. Kathy was the very best friend I could possibly have had. When the going got tough, you went to Kathy. I relied on her for so many things, I don't know what I'm going to do without her in my life.

"Best of all, Kathy was a wonderful mother. She taught our sons to be strong and free. She taught them to be proud of themselves. To care for others. She got involved in all their activities, including softball practices, hockey practices, things a few years ago she had never done in her life. Tanner and Shea cherished their mother.

"I came across a poem the other day that reminds me so

much of Kathy that I would like to share it with you. It's called 'Of Mountains and Women.'

The hearts of mountains
and the hearts of women
are both the same.
They beat to an old rhythm,
an old song.

Mountains and women are made
from the sinew of the rock.
Mountains and women are home
to the spirits of the earth.
Mountains and women are created
with beauty all around.

Mountains and women embrace
the mystery of life.
Mountains give patience to women;
women give fullness to mountains.

Celebrate each mountain, each woman.
Sing songs to mountains and to women,
dance for them in your dreams.

The spirit of mountains and women
will give courage to our children
long after we are gone.

"Kathy, Kathy, Kathy. I loved you so very much. Please guide me and be with me the rest of my life.

"Tanner Arthur Daily was our oldest. He was so wise and gentle and sensitive and happy. Tanner always had a smile on his face. And like his mom, he was funny. One of the things I loved best about Tanner was his absolute willingness to encourage himself, to say to himself, 'I am the best little guy that I can possibly be!' He had a powerful spirit. He was one of the smallest boys on his hockey team, but he never let it slow him down. In the game he played last Saturday, when a guy twice his size came charging across the blue line with the puck, Tanner just stepped up and took him out of the play. And like his mom, Tanner was a great friend. All you young guys and girls who were close to Tanner, he loved all of you very much. His friendships with you meant everything to him. Tanner wrote a poem about himself that maybe describes him best of all.

ME

Tanner.
Funny. Smart. Creative. Athletic.
   Brother of Shea.
Who feels weird, cool, ridiculous.
Who needs a new hockey stick,
   air walks, hockey pads.
Who fears beetles, barracudas, sharks.
Who gives food, love, friendship.
Who loves family, cats, dogs.

> Who would like to see Nepal,
> the Bahamas, Los Angeles.
> Resident of Aspen.

"Tanner also wrote a poem about death and hope. I'd like to share that with you, too.

FACES

> At night I look out my window and see
> a million faces looking down at me.
> Each represents a different face,
> a different thing or a different race.
> So every time a thing dies,
> and every time a face grows sad
> and falls across the sky,
> it falls into a newborn living thing
> and becomes part of its race.

"Shea Rider Daily was our little one. He was so special. He was an old soul who had a wonderful understanding of people. We called him Shea-mon. He was a mischievous elf. The outlaw of the family. And often, when it came down to how things were going to get done, it was Shea's way or the highway. Lord knows where he learned that.

"Somehow, Shea was born to be my heart, my soul. No matter where I was or what I was doing, Shea wanted to be part of me. He was a second heart beating inside me, alongside my own. He had bad dreams sometimes, so every night when I put him to bed, I'd rub his back and count his backbones like my dad used to count mine, and I'd do what we called 'doing his dreams.' Shea would say, 'Hey Dad, do my dreams,' which was this great ritual where I'd sing to him about how he was going to have the most wonderful dreams that he'd ever had. And then later on, most nights, about 2:00 a.m., I'd hear the click of the bedroom door opening and closing and a minute later Shea would be standing next to me with his blanket, waiting to be lifted into bed. And then he'd snuggle up next to me and go back to sleep. I looked forward to hearing the click of that door.

"Shea and Tanner were incredibly close for boys over four years apart. They loved each other so very deeply. They were proud and protective of each other. As you can tell, I loved my sons with everything I had. I can't begin to describe the pain of losing them.

"I'm not really sure what to believe about where Kathy, Shea, and Tanner are now. But the answer to that question is desperately important to me. I'm going to work on it, and I'm going to try to get as clear about it as I can. What do I want to believe? What do I hope? Most important, that they are together, that they are part of a perfect peace and joy. And that with their perfect love, they care about how we are doing. That they are holding me right now in their arms. And most of all, I hope that when my time is done, I'm going to be with them again. That has to be true.

"Many of you have read the book Kathy wrote recently with Gaylord about Aspen's quiet years, about that time between 1900 and 1940 when less than seven hundred fifty people were living in Aspen. It was tough as hell to make a living. One of the common threads that ran through the stories of the old-timers Kathy interviewed was that no matter how desperate things got, the people in Aspen never lost their sense of community. When somebody needed help, everybody showed up. People took care of each other and that caring was one of the vital things that kept the town alive.

"I want all of you to know that the outpouring of love that I have received from you over the past several days has proven to me beyond any doubt that Aspen has not lost that vital quality.

"The other day I was shown a medallion that is given to people in AA who have stayed sober for a period of time. The medallion contains the following words:

> I sought my God, and he eluded me.
> I sought my soul, and it I could not see.
> I sought my brother, and I found all three.

"You are my brothers, you are my sisters. I could not be standing here if I did not have your support. From the bottom of my heart, thanks for being here with me. Please God, bless us all."

I walk away from the lectern and stand alone, facing the gathering. Unbidden, John leaves his seat and comes up the stairs to stand with me. A few parting words are spoken, musicians Jimmy Ibbotson and Bobby Mason lead "Amazing Grace," and the service is over. People stand quietly as I walk with Piper and John and his family up the crowded aisle and out the doors into the fading light of late afternoon.

The reception is across a field at the Aspen Meadows conference center, and as I enter the foyer friends stop me with hugs, and kind words, and sometimes a searching quietness. There is respect for each person's time with me, and a line forms that extends across the hall and down a staircase and beyond. They feel my desolation, my aloneness, and they lay their hands on me to change that a little, if only for a moment. Each touch is meant as a small voice of hope, and I know now what I could not know then, that these moments in the embrace of so many other human beings are the first steps of a long journey. I am surrounded and lifted by compassion, and I never move beyond the place where I first stop, just inside the front door.

At some point two men approach me. One is a venerable and beloved doctor in town, and the other a tall, slim younger man I don't know. The stranger introduces himself as Steve Hinckey. They have waited in line a long time to tell me that they were driving home through Glenwood Canyon shortly after the accident occurred. Cars were being allowed through in a single lane, and as they drove slowly by they saw me by the side of the road with the boys and they wondered if they could help. Steve quietly tells me that he observed three small globes of light emerge from the accident scene and rise slowly together up the wall of the canyon and on into the darkening sky. The men knew then that they could not make a difference, and they moved on. Steve goes on to say to me, "Art, I don't know if any of this makes sense to you, but somehow you and I were meant to meet at this time. I do chiropractic healing work in a little studio outside of town, and I'd like to spend some time with you when you're ready." I don't have any experience with this sort of thing, but I'm drawn by the man's unusual spirit, and I glimpse the shadow of an awareness that who I have been in the past will not be enough in the time ahead.

Another memorial service is held a few days later at the Aspen Ice Garden, for all the kids in the Aspen Junior Hockey program. Tanner and Shea's coaches speak, as does one of Kathy's team members on the Aspen Mother Puckers, a top women's team in Colorado. I talk to the young players about how much the game of hockey meant to my family, and how much I appreciated their friendship with my sons. Kathy's teammate reminisces about Kathy's wonderful approach to trying to learn how to skate and play hockey the previous year at forty-seven years old—Kathy wasn't very good, but she did everything possible to get better, and she took immense joy in simply participating. She didn't get much time on the ice with the Mother Puckers, but she knew the secret: she was there for the joy of hockey; she was there just to play.

Aspen Junior Hockey retires the boys' jerseys, and two Squirts and then two Mites take either end of a pole and skate their jerseys around the ice. Many of them are deeply wounded, and the ceremony is performed slowly and quietly. My heart breaks again as I watch these children saying good-bye to their friends. As I turn from the ice I find that a few old friends of mine who could not reach Aspen in time for the service at Harris Hall have come to the Ice Garden. Among them are Piper's mother, who has flown a long way to be with Piper in this time and whom I still cherish as a friend, and a woman who has left her own boys in Steamboat for the afternoon to tell me she is saddened by my loss. We shared a summer together in the mid-1960s, when I was working construction in the mountains above Grand Lake, and our lives moved on in different directions. I am touched that they are here.

Passing into the Cave

MY FAMILY AND FRIENDS RETURN TO THEIR OWN LIVES, AND I must find my way. I know it comes down to that, but I don't seem very well equipped. Who am I? To what do I turn in this barren time? My truth, my soul elude me, and I'm beginning to realize that I've never known them very well. Piper remains with me, and we talk about these things, these dim pathways that are opening before me. Sorrow and despair are my intimate companions, and it would be so easy to cloak myself in them, to descend into them, to become my grief. My friends will understand, surely, if I feel sorry for myself for a while. I'm entitled to that. My soul may slowly wither away, but does it really matter? Or I can do battle with myself. I can find a way to open my heart and live again. I was not meant to die in the accident, and some elemental part of me doesn't want to quit now. My angels are emerging. Quiet voices seem to be saying, over and over, "Choose life, Art. Reach for it." Yet I don't know how.

There are no road maps for this journey, and all I know in

my heart is that I must keep faith, that I must continue to protect the ones that I love, even though they are gone. At the close of *Memoir from Antproof Case*, Mark Helprin says, "The first songs are the gentlest and the most beautiful, they last forever, and they are the test of faith. You learn, and sometimes as I did, you learn early, that love can overcome death, and that what is required of you in this is memory and devotion. Memory and devotion. To keep your love alive you must be willing to be obstinate, and irrational, and true, to fashion your entire life as a construct, a metaphor, a fiction, a device for the exercise of faith. Without this, you will live like a beast and have nothing but an aching heart. With it, your heart, though broken, will be full, and you will stay in the fight unto the very last."

Such perfect words. They resonate within me, and speak the thoughts that I am unable to form. This is where I must go. It is my destiny now. To continue to love and honor and protect Kathy, Tanner, and Shea, to live out my life with faith and devotion.

Morning, noon, and night I am consumed with desperate grief, with a terrible longing for them. At times, while driving, I pull over to the side of the road and scream and scream out my anger and pain, crying so hopelessly that I cannot breathe. I wonder if anyone sees this and is afraid for me. I carry small pictures of my family with me. I see them everywhere, in clouds and animals and in flights of birds and butterflies. I glimpse them in shadows and reflections and in crowds of people that I don't know. And I feel them within me and around me, particularly in our house when there is an electrical charge in the air, or movement in the corners of my eyes, or inexplicable sounds from empty rooms. I don't know what to do with these experiences. My whole being wants them to be real, to have my boys and my woman continue to be present in my life. To hold me and play with me, argue and fight with me, and hurt me and love me, and me them, the way it was.

But the sane part of me knows that it cannot be, and so I make do with what I have: my imagination, my dreams, my rampant, naked feelings, my unleashed wonder. I can't tell what is really there from what is there only because I so much want it to be. My personal frames of reference are useless to me, and my familiar world has become a wilderness of knowing and unknowing, of holding tight to the few parts of me that are still anchored to something logical, and I'm increasingly finding that I must let go. I have lived in control, and in the end it didn't make any difference. The power wasn't mine; it rested elsewhere. I'm going to have to learn to live with the uncertainness and to trust in something beyond all of this. My loved ones are still with me, and they will be always. It is enough for now. Knowing this, I can go on.

I begin to return to my office, my work. I have fine partners, a caring staff, and it's a good place to be. My real estate development practice is challenging, and I find that it means a lot to return to this haven. It occupies my mind, for short periods at first and eventually for a longer time, so that I am not focused inward every moment of the day. Boots, my partner and sidekick from the wild years of the 1970s and early '80s, checks in somehow at the right times, fearlessly and thoughtfully. A bit of a loner, he runs deep and true. I am blessed by his friendship, especially now. This law work is not just a part of my past. I realize that I will stay with it, and I sense even now that, of necessity, I will bring a greater intensity and compassion to the work that I do.

During the week following the service I drive to the mortuary in Glenwood Springs to pick up the urns I have chosen. I haven't given much thought yet to what to do with the ashes, and Piper builds a pretty shrine around the urns on Kathy's desk. Pictures, personal things. A comforting place to spend a few quiet minutes. I call the grade school and ask Tanner and Shea's teachers if it would be helpful to the boys' classmates if I came by to see them. They welcome the idea, so I schedule an hour with each group. The night before visiting Shea's first grade class I sit in the boys' room wondering if there are any things of Shea's that I can take to his friends. Suddenly I notice his beloved collection of small furry animals, and I put most of them in a plastic bag to take to the school, keeping a couple of his favorites at home. I let each of his classmates choose an animal, saying it is Shea's gift, and they clutch them to their breasts with soft eyes. We sit on the floor together, one or two always in my lap, and we talk about many things. They feel my sorrow and would change it if they could. They are sweet beings, and I'm glad I have come. Years have since gone by, and these children are growing up, but their parents tell me that their sons and daughters still cherish the little stuffed toys that belonged to their friend Shea.

I am less easy about visiting Tanner's fifth grade class. These kids are more worldly, more articulate, and they understand better what has happened. I have nothing of Tanner's to take to them, so I just show up and we arrange ourselves in a big circle on the floor. Some of Tanner's closest boy buddies are in this group, as are two girls that he liked a lot. They have thought about the accident, they've tried to imagine it, but they weren't there and they are haunted by what they don't know. The teacher asks me if it would be all right if each child asks me a question. With some trepidation, I say, "I would like that." The questions are piercing. "What did Tanner look like?" "Was he bleeding?" "Was he awake, in pain, crying?" "How did he die?" "Could you have avoided the boulder?" I answer each child as directly and truthfully as I can, tears in my eyes, holding their hands. They need to know. These children, too, want to be close to me, to touch me. Their young spirits are stronger than mine; they are comfortable being close to the pain. Maybe I have softened some of their fears. I know they have helped me with my own.

Being Here Now

I CONTINUE TO RECEIVE DOZENS OF LETTERS AND CARDS EACH day, in the end many hundreds of them, from people near to me and others I will never meet. All are messages of kindness, of caring, of concern. The writers want to help in any way they can. That is what their words are for, to let me know that they, too, are hurt and confused by this tragedy, that they will be there for me if I need them. Some share with me stories of great losses in their own lives and how they have survived them, in the hope that I will find some meaning there. A surprising number send poems and sometimes even books, about grief and loss, on surviving the death of a child, on life after death, about mystery and angels and miracles. Every letter and every memory matters. I am slightly less alone; I float a little higher in the water. I find that I'm unwilling to just skip through these writings. I need to spend time with each of them, however long or short, however intimate or distant the words. I owe it to the person who sat down to share something with me, and I owe it to myself. They are messages of hope, and they are part of the way back. So I read eight or ten a day, and at night I read the books and poems, and sometimes I talk to Piper about them.

Of the many beautiful letters, one stands out in my memory. A man I do not know writes to me from Seattle to tell me about what happened to him during 1944 in war-torn Europe, for such consolation as I may make of it. He was piloting a B-17 bomber in a raid over Germany when his plane was shot down. During the battle all contact with other crew members was lost, and when the aircraft was irretrievably broken and would no longer fly he parachuted away and became a POW for the remainder of the war. When he was freed, he learned that all but four of the other thirteen crew members had perished in the bomber, and throughout the fifty years since he has continued to ask himself over and over again the same question, "Why me? Why did I survive, when other splendid young men did not?" He told me that while he never came to a satisfactory answer, he did come to terms with himself by devoting a good part of his life toward preventing a recurrence of another great war, by giving aid to disabled veterans, and by adopting and raising three fine young men. He closed with the following reflection: "While I have few illusions about my life, I have tried to make a difference where I could. In a very real sense, the loss of my dear friends on that January day in 1944 has sustained me and strengthened my resolve to make my life count for something." These powerful words have remained with me and have helped to guide me in my journey. They explain, maybe better than I can, why I am writing this story. For my children. And to make a difference.

I was moved, too, by the simplest lines from a poem given to me by a friend, "On Angels" by Czesław Miłosz. After confirming the existence of angels, the poet describes the message that the angels have for us, in our times of fury and pain and doubt:

> day draws near
> another one
> do what you can.

I have repeated these words, in my own way, a thousand times since those early days. They define as well as anything how I have continued to move forward. The dawn comes, each day, however much I try to hold on to the darkness. I learn to expect, and to be content with, only what I am able to do that day, nothing more but nothing less.

One day I receive a call from a woman I know in the valley, who tells me that Steve Hinckey, the chiropractor, has been trying to reach me. I haven't had much time for the phone, and I've missed his messages. I remember our conversation at the reception, and I dial the number she has given me. Steve answers and says he has been thinking about me a lot and invites me to come out to his place to experience the healing work he is doing. Since I really don't understand what I'm feeling most of the time or where I'm going or what to do next, I decide that it can't do any harm to meet with him.

When I arrive, there are twelve or fifteen massage tables scattered about his small studio, about half of them occupied by people lying quietly with their eyes closed. Steve is moving slowly from one to another, reading spinal energy with his fingers, making small adjustments, and occasionally realigning someone's neck. He invites me to take off my shoes and lie down on one of the tables, and he begins to examine my own locked-up body. The shadowy environment is soothing. Candlelit, there is a deep and respectful stillness, and a low meditative chanting somewhere beyond it all. Steve talks quietly to himself and sometimes shares with me a little of what my body is telling him. Unexpectedly, a sense of peacefulness comes over me, and for the first time since the accident I begin to float free of the thoughts and emotions that haunt me. My body relaxes and my mind stills, I am oddly free of self-consciousness, and for a while I just enjoy being there. I've never done much healing work before, but I will return to this man often over the next few months. At times his touch will bring forth gut-wrenching crying that comes from some bottomless place, without warning or explanation. At others I just drift in the moment, absorbed in the chanting, in the remote chimes, in the resonance of the om. Somehow he is helping the healing to begin, the mending of the shattered fragments of myself.

Piper joins me sometimes, but usually I go alone. I start to recognize some of the other people who come to Steve, and

I am struck by the aura of tranquillity that surrounds many of them. The collective energy in the room is powerful, and it seems to merge with my own, to lift me, to free me. While I don't understand it very well, there is something here that I need, that is working for me. I ask Steve where I can obtain the chanting tapes that I enjoy the most, and I order several. Piper and I listen to them in the evening at home, on the floor of my bedroom, sometimes with headphones. They are ancient voices, echoing the sounds of the world before the time of men, and they release the spirit. Steve also gives us his last two copies of an extraordinary poster, depicting the face of a wild and powerful man who is bursting with laughter. "The Laughing Christ" has been hanging next to my bed ever since.

Aspen's mayor calls. We've been casual acquaintances for many years, and he tells me that Baba Ram Dass is conducting a spiritual workshop at the Hotel Jerome during the coming weekend and that two tickets have been left at the door for Piper and me in case we want to attend. I remember Ram Dass from the early 1970s, when I used to roll a fat doobie and read his classic *Be Here Now* by candlelight in my small garret bedroom in the house I was renting on the east end of town. Piper's mother had recently left me, and I was lonely and looking around for signs of where I was. Ram Dass took me on a joyful journey into myself, beseeching me to be fully present in my life, and I came away feeling like a larger, warmer being, maybe even a little bit enlightened. This was not my usual state, and I've always been grateful to Ram Dass for attempting to teach a meaningful way of living to our restless, passionate generation. Not having any plans for the weekend, or for any other weekend for the rest of my life, I ask Piper if she wants to go. She says, "If you think it'll be worthwhile, let's do it."

The ballroom at the Jerome is beginning to fill up as we arrive, and the several hundred of us in attendance settle ourselves on cushions at the edge of the raised dais. Ram Dass walks onto the stage, blessing us with an outlaw's smile and twinkling eyes, radiating inner peace. Like the rest of us, he is older now, but his voice and spirit are strong. He leads us in meditations and chants and dances, and he talks to us of the purpose and peace and eternal wisdom that live within us all. Many of those present know of the accident, and they nod softly to me from across the room or touch me in passing, happy that I am here. It feels good to be looking inward while surrounded by others, and once again I find myself enjoying the newness of the experience. Without really understanding it, I am doing what I need to be doing, and the lonesomeness and bitterness and self-pity retreat for a time. Everything I do in this room seems to bring Tanner and Shea and Kathy closer to me, and in the moments when I am most fully present I feel one or another of them speaking to me in a language that I seem to have always known.

At the start of the lunch break on Friday, Ram Dass surprises me by walking over to stand with Piper and me for a few minutes. I tell him my name, and he gives me a long hug and says, "Art, you didn't need to introduce yourself. There is an aura, an openness that shines about you. You've been terribly wounded, and I would like to be of some comfort to you if I can. If you're free on Sunday morning, we could spend time together." I tell him that I would be honored to be with him, and he asks me to pick him up at eight in front of the Jerome.

Sunday arrives glittering cold and clear, and as Ram Dass climbs into the car he suggests that we drive over to my house. We sit down in the family room, on the new couch Kathy had ordered before the accident, and Ram Dass says, "Bring over some pictures of your family. Let's all be here together." The house is full of photographs, and I gather my favorites and place them on the table in front of us. We look at them in silence, and my family becomes so present and so real that I just fall apart in front of Ram Dass. I am crying blindly, uncontrollably, and Dass is simply there with me. I know that he spends much of his time with the dying. Compassion and understanding shine about him. I am in the presence of someone who knows a lot about God.

He begins to tell me of the transformations that took place in him during the 1960s, inspired by psilocybin mushrooms and by his guru, Neem Karoli Baba, known as Maharaji. He explains that as he became familiar with other planes of consciousness, he came to see that "there is much more in any given moment than we usually perceive, and we ourselves are much more than we usually perceive." Maharaji has been dead for many years now, but for Ram Dass he has remained fully present. Dass talks to me of his absolute faith, of his intimate experience, that Maharaji is as much here now as he was before his death. He wants me to understand, and he tells me over and over in different ways that this is not merely a belief or a longing of the heart but a complete and perfect truth. Maharaji exists in a different form but he is still alive, he is still here, and he is a vital part of Ram Dass's life. They communicate with one another as easily as they did before his death.

Dass takes my hands and looks into me for a while, and then quietly but clearly says to me, "Art, what my guru taught me, and what I came here to share with you today, is that faith and love are stronger than death and that death is not what it appears. You know in your soul that Tanner and Kathy and Shea are still with you; you have been experiencing their presence, their love, and their guidance since shortly after the accident. Open yourself to this truth, and remain open to it, because it will always be so. And they will be waiting for you when it is your time."

It is one of the greatest gifts that I will ever receive. To hear these things from this dedicated man, to experience the power of his absolute knowledge of Kathy, Shea, and Tanner's presence, seems to strip away the strangeness of believing in them, the fear that they are merely my imagination, my hope. As I sit there with him, I feel myself becoming one with them again. A great peace comes over me and I am bathed in a sweet and gentle love.

The following day I sit down at the old Santa Fe Railroad desk in Kathy's study, open up a new volume of *Aspen: The Quiet Years*, and write a long inscription of appreciation inside the flyleaf. I sign it, "With our love, Art and Kathy and Tanner and Shea," and mail it off to Ram Dass. It is all that I have to give him, and yet it also seems the best thing.

As my life slowly begins again, nothing is as it was before. I'm not aware of actively seeking change; indeed, my nature is to surround myself with the familiar, to stay in the comfort zone. Yet some part of me has become pure light, and I seem drawn to unusual people and experiences by an invisible force. Deborah, our old pal who leads vision quests in the desert, suggests that Piper and I join her in a group that gathers on Tuesday evenings in a small art studio to chant together. I've always loved singing, but I really haven't done very much of it in my life. I sang in an Episcopalian choir for years as a boy, and I sang songs and poems to Tanner and Shea every night while putting them to bed. Chanting is a different deal; I've only just started to listen to chants and now I'm singing them. I'm the only man in a group of seven or eight women, and we sit in a circle in a room lit by candles. One of the women is the lead singer in a local blues band, several others have beautiful voices, and they lead us in a series of Hindu chants that take us to another place, another time. My connections with the world and the spirit are badly broken. The chanting is strangely inspiring and nurturing; my spirit rises up and out and seems to float free from its moorings, and for those short times I am happy again. During the chanting I feel connected to something larger, something eternal and divine, and I am grateful.

One of these nights we see a poster about a group of Sufi dancers who are coming to town for an evening, and Piper and I end up going. They dance in inner and outer circles, moving joyfully and gracefully and chanting, and they make us all part of it. I'm surprised, once again, by how much I enjoy myself. My old belief systems have been shattered, and the wildest things come along to fill the emptiness.

Deborah also introduces us to a woman who teaches meditation, which is something else I know nothing about. Piper and Deborah and I form a small class and practice meditation once or twice a week for a couple of months. I have my own mantra, and I actually participate in a graduation ceremony of sorts, but meditation doesn't seem to be my calling. There is a restfulness and a self-discipline in it that I find appealing, but it feels like I am meant to be fully present in a different way.

One day at the office I receive in the mail an envelope containing an oval earring of translucent green Italian glass, etched in intaglio and bordered in gold. It is one of a pair that I gave to Kathy at Christmas. An unsigned note accompanies it: "While investigating the accident site, I found this earring on the side of the highway. If it belonged to your wife, it now belongs with you. I'm so terribly sorry for your loss." I sit at my desk crying, remembering Kathy wearing the earrings, quietly proud of them. I hold it in my hand for a while, looking at it, sensing its purpose, and finally I walk across town to a jeweler acquaintance who works in gold. I ask him if he can turn the earring into a pendant, and when he says he can, I choose a small braided gold chain, try it on for length and leave everything with him. I pick it up a few days later, the earring now fixed with a gold loop for the chain, and I clasp the chain behind my neck. Other than a wristwatch, I don't have any jewelry, but this looks and feels as if it has always been a part of me. Some things don't require explanation, and I have never taken it off. I'm beginning to understand that Kathy intends to continue to play an important role in my life, but she knows that I may not be able to hear her as well as others do. The earring is a tangible presence, a reminder that Kathy and the boys are always next to my heart. I can see them more clearly when I hold it.

Clawing Back from the Darkness

I'M ENJOYING TRYING ON NEW THINGS, BUT MY SPIRIT IS IN A lot of trouble. I feel like Iron Hans at the bottom of his emerald pool, hoping for deliverance. Am I waiting for Godot? I don't understand what is happening to me, and I can't tell whether I'm treading water or slowly dying inside. I am really lost, and I'm becoming aware that I can't heal alone, that I need serious help. My mind has normally been reasonably sound, and I've never met professionally with a psychiatrist or a psychologist. Having no idea what I'm looking for but hoping that I'll know it when I find it, I set about interviewing local psychiatrists who have been recommended to me. I like and respect them all, but a vital resonance is missing. Eventually I make an appointment with Brad Ham, the clinical psychologist friend of Edgell's, the one I had poured my heart out to the morning of the service. I don't know why I hadn't thought of him sooner.

It is intimate experience that has led Brad to specialize in grief and loss counseling. He tells me that some years ago he lost a beloved wife and unborn son to illness, and that it almost killed him. Instead of honoring the pain and anger and loneliness, instead of running with the hounds of loss, he immersed himself in his theological studies. Shortly after receiving his doctorate, he noticed on a church bulletin board a small Eskimo tribe's plea for assistance in protecting their sovereignty from encroachment by the Alaskan government. The letter had been floating around the ministry for several years. The tribe lived alone on a remote island in the Bering Strait, and Brad flew in by float plane to see if he could be of help. They were a primitive people who had almost no contact with the outside world, and they lived on fish and walrus and an occasional whale that they caught on the ice floes that extended out into the strait. A sister tribe speaking the same language occupied a village on the Russian Kamchatka Peninsula, some eighteen miles across the strait.

Brad ended up spending several uncommon years on their island. The grief that he had so long neglected caught up with him, and he found himself in a place of deep emotional darkness. An old Eskimo woman recognized his spiritual pain and took charge of him, gradually guiding him back to the light. Other tribe members, some of them shamans, showed Brad how they could will their physical beings through the air from one place to another, much as the Yaqui *brujos* had demonstrated to Carlos Castaneda. They would use this skill to travel far out onto the ice floes, and Brad was told that sometimes a tribe member would travel across the strait to visit kinfolk on the Russian shore. They were a harsh and strangely

caring people, governed by ancient beliefs and by wisdom forgotten by the rest of our world.

Brad has stories of experiences in other faraway places,
of being charged by grizzlies and surviving great storms, and
he seems to me a living testament to the existence of miracles. Since I find myself in a state of awe and wonder—that I
am suddenly so alone, that I am alive, that I am in despair,
that sometimes I feel a glow of light about me—Brad is clearly
the man for me, and I will continue to see him for the next eighteen months. I tell him things that I've never spoken about
before; I talk of things that I am not aware that I know. I understand now what it means to be a stranger in a strange land.
I'm discovering who I am. I have had a glimpse of the infinite.
I scream in sheer madness and horror of my vanished family,
and Brad softly encourages me to stay with the anguish, the
torment, to experience it again and again for as long as my
soul needs to cry. Sometimes he holds me in his strong embrace
as I sob uncontrollably; sometimes we cry together. There are
no battle plans for this engagement, no maps of this alien
space, and my emotions run wildly down dark and unknown
courses. I am going to survive this, I can feel that now, but
sometimes I am very afraid of what I cannot see ahead.

For a number of years I have gotten aerobic exercise in
the winter by snowshoeing up the mountains that surround
Aspen. I usually participate in America's Uphill, an annual
town race up the face of Aspen Mountain that starts at 7:00
a.m. on a Saturday in March, but most of the time I walk up
Buttermilk Mountain and catch a free ride on the ski lift back

to the bottom. The hike up takes less than an hour, and I've found that it's a great way to break up a stressful workday, to clear my mind and give my emotions some breathing room. I had actually taken the Buttermilk hike in the early morning the day of the accident, to get my blood flowing before driving to Vail. I remember being startled by a couple of magpies that flew across the slope in front of me as I started up the hill, because one of them was flying upside down. I've heard that birds know when things are going to happen. Perhaps the magpie was trying to tell me something. I know I've never seen one fly upside down, either before or since.

Several weeks after the accident I begin to snowshoe again, and I find that once I break through the resistance of preferring to stay huddled in my sorrow, the workout and the fresh air and the beauty of my surroundings are wonderfully cleansing. My mind and my emotions gradually lift out of their bleakness, and fresh thoughts and feelings begin to emerge. It helps me to feel more alive, and I find myself starting to think of the future again, tentatively at first and then with increasing faith. I vividly recall one ride down on the lift in late March—probably a month after the accident—when I am feeling the terrible emptiness of not having any young children to give my love to, to raise and teach and share with. For the first time I begin evaluating my prospects for having more children in my life. For all the obvious reasons, not the least being that I'm fifty-four years old, I've had a vasectomy, and the women I know well are all friends, not potential mates, there seems little likelihood that I will father any more children of my own. And for most of the same reasons, I am not much of a candidate to be an adoptive father. I can join the Buddy Program and become a mentor to a child who doesn't have a father, and I think that maybe I'll do that when more time has gone by, but I am deeply saddened by this awareness. My greatest passion, my truest joy, is being a father. I don't know what I'm going to do or who I'm going to be without that.

A Far Voice

While Art is on Buttermilk Mountain wondering what his future holds, I am in my house listening to music. Music is what heals me. It takes my heart and soul to places I've never been before. Music got me through my brother's suicide four years ago; it eased the depression I experienced in my divorce two years later. There's never just one kind of music but always a variety. Today it's Bette Midler—I can't say why. I am feeling alone and melancholy, wondering where my life is going. I turn up the volume and allow Bette's rich voice to permeate my soul. At twenty-eight, I feel lost, alone, and drifting; the lyrics give me permission to go there, knowing I will come back. I have no passion at the time, no place to direct my energy. Spring has arrived, and I will be leaving Colorado soon to begin a new job in Dallas. I'm not sad, just alone with myself and the music.

The story of my winter in Aspen begins back in early December. It's a pretty day in Austin, and my college friend Kat and I are packing up a U-Haul full of our junk, hooking it up to her Explorer, and putting all of our favorite tapes of songs in the front seat to fight over what artist comes next. We smile at one another as we load up the last of our things, and Kat turns and says to me, "Allison, we need to do this; we deserve this time." We are two girls on a mission—to do something we've never done before. We both have been "good girls" our whole lives. Now we are going to be irresponsible, live on the edge, and not be so predictable.

We sing all the way out of Austin and into the hills. The mountains are beckoning. All of the baggage we have been carrying is no longer weighing us down. We talk about our pain and then let it go, as if the long road ahead is washing away the tears.

My divorce is behind me. I still feel guilt and so I continue to talk about all that Duncan did wrong to cause me to leave. I'm still blind to the fact that, mostly, it was me. It was my pain from losing my oldest brother Rod, my wake-up call. When Rod took the gun to his head, the part of me that thought my life had been perfect was shot as well. The Barbie dolls with the perfect clothes, the perfect body, and the perfect life—the one I was striving for—all of a sudden shattered. I had built a mask, a shield, over my whole body. It had become my reality and it had looked and felt right to me. I was a tennis pro, a devoted Christian, an attractive woman who was marrying a very handsome Christian tennis pro. The suppressed rage and ugliness that came out of me six months after Rod's death and four months into our marriage were terrifying. In the privacy of our home, after I had kept the image of our perfect life of tennis pros at the country club intact, I would taunt Duncan into a fight and end up yelling at and sometimes hitting him. I became four years old again. I wanted someone to take control, to hold me, to break this glass, this work of art that I had sculpted around me. I was tired and sad and alone. I had lived in a state of fear as long as I could remember. I had made choices based on what looked good, afraid I would be rejected if I didn't live up to others' and my own expectations. It wasn't until the marriage fell apart and I opened up to my therapist that I began to admit how sick my behavior was.

I watch Kat driving and wonder what she is thinking. I don't ask because the silence is too precious. I open the car window and allow cold air to blow my hair in every direction. I silently pray for the anxiety, apprehension, and depression to fly away. I want to heal. I lean over and stick my head out. I want the wind to take with it the parts of me that I hate. I want it to be that easy, that simple. I want to stop hating myself.

Kat also lost her brother, her closest friend, when he died in his sleep when they were young. The cause of death was never determined and I'm sure she fears sleep every night. When I lost Rod, the pain Kat and I shared brought us even closer.

"I hope there is joy out there for both of us. It's time," I say.

As we drive through Aspen and up Independence Pass to the house we will spend the winter in, I can feel the peace around us. It's like entering another world, a forest of possibility. The snow is vividly white and the air so clean that my nostrils hurt. The mountains invite me to heal as I stare in awe, my hand over my heart; the snow that covers them is a blanket of protection.

We stop the car to get out and I feel inside like a small hill, a bump in the road that has no covering and no beauty. I have failed at a marriage, I'm raw from digging into my brother's suicide, and I have no idea what I can give back to this world. I want to learn to love myself, even the bad parts. I went cold turkey off my antidepressant when we left Austin. I decided if I was going to stop living in fear I was going to stop covering up so much of the pain. The drugs have served their purpose. I know if I want to love myself I need to get a close look at who I am.

The old house we are renting is sectioned off into three parts for three sets of tenants. It is organic and earthy, like living inside a tree. The man who built it did so literally around the environment. The trees come into the house and out through the roof. The furniture and amenities are rustic and basic. It's cold from all the windows and cracks leading to the outside that will never be filled in. The solid wood bathtub is built for a Big Foot, and hot water, as we find out, is a rarity. In the same room as the bathtub is a big slushy water bed. You feel you are out at sea every time you sit on it. We decide to trade off sleeping there.

There is old drug paraphernalia all over our portion of the house. Neither Kat nor I have done any drugs (we are good girls, remember) and aren't quite sure what the devices are for. Our two sets of neighbors who share the house come over to introduce themselves and quickly show us. We both stare in amazement.

Our housemates are seven boys who have just graduated from the University of Colorado and are here to party, ski every day, and attempt to work in order to support their wild lifestyles until they enter the real world. They are roughly six years younger than us and are great looking, fun, and interesting. All seven become our brothers, although at times, usually after heavy drinking, one of them will attempt to cross the line. Their goal is to have us smoke pot, which is an everyday ritual for most of them, and our goal is to wean them off. Neither side wins. Instead we take care of them in the mornings after nights when the party bug gets out of hand.

Kat and I scrape plates and clean tables at the Sundeck Restaurant on top of Aspen Mountain during the day, and we are cocktail waitresses at the Chart House downtown at night. We ski, hike, and work. Life is simple in a "cozy, curl up in a blanket" sort of way. Each morning we come out of our rooms wrapped in a comforter to stay warm. Many a morning is spent with my hands wrapped around a coffee cup, allowing myself to wake up while looking out the big, long living-room windows at the wild preserve outside.

One morning in late February, after greeting Kat, I sit in stillness while she studies on the opposite couch for her GRE exam. I wonder if I'll see the giant elk that occasionally visits in the open field. The snow drips off the barren branches; occasionally a big clump will fall, upsetting the smaller branches. The more frail branches seem to cry out as the wood crackles from the heavier snow. Then it is quiet again. Kat has gone to shower and ski before work. Time slows down. The aloneness, the solitude within me isn't so alarming. I am beginning to see that this is how the land and mountains are healing me. They are a mirror, a witness for me. As I observe their peace, maybe I can find my own.

I go make a second cup of coffee. The smell alone is a grace. Kat has left and I let the tears fall. I know my outward appearance of happiness and energy is only a cover to the emotions stuck in my throat. It is my only defense. If I can pretend I'm happy while I work, I can almost feel what the real thing must be like. I had thought for so long that I knew what joy and peace were. Now I am redefining these emotions in myself. Contemplating Rod's suicide has opened up a Pandora's box in me that desperately needs unwrapping. I don't know who I am anymore—I am not the strong Christian, the nice-looking tennis pro, the bubbly daughter. I am just a face in the crowd. Here no one knows me except for Kat, and she is on her own similar journey. At night I cry and cry. Waking to these big windows, filled with mountains and untouched land, is a comfort. The hollowness is now a friend, I think, as I get up to answer the phone.

A few hours later, Kat is wiping off the bar tables at the Chart House, setting up for work. "Kat, Peepaw died. I just got the call before I came. I'm leaving tomorrow for Texas. I'll stay a week. I've cleared it with work." She stops what she is doing and looks at me.

"I'm sorry," she says. "I'll cover anything you need."

"Thanks." We smile. Throughout the evening as we stop at the bar station for more drinks, she puts her hand on mine.

Letter from a Stranger

I've returned from my grandfather's funeral. Once again I'm sitting in my cozy Aspen home gazing out the window and listening to music. My thoughts drift to the man who lost his family in Glenwood Canyon while I was gone. His name is Art. People who know him whom I work with at the Chart House are still shaken by the accident. I think that my aloneness is nothing compared to his. I begin praying for him. I don't know why, really, only that I hoped someone was praying for me when my brother died. As the music plays, an idea comes to me. I begin to make a tape of songs for this man to help him grieve. I pull out all my tapes and CDs and spread them on the floor. I remember lyrics to certain songs, and I pick ones that will touch his pain, allow him to feel it and heal. Each song I copy speaks to me, telling me it is the one. Hours go by. I cry for him, allowing my own pain to surface. While I am finishing the tape, I find myself talking to God, asking him to give me some of this man's pain.

The next day I use a guest pass someone has given me to go up to the Aspen Club to work out in the gym. As I work on one of the weight machines I overhear a conversation between two men who are standing nearby. They're talking about the accident, and as I shift subtly around in their direction I recognize Art from the pictures in the paper following his family's service. Their voices are soft, but the conversation is somber. I quickly finish my workout and head for the steam room, feeling a little off balance because of the connection I feel to this man I've never met. As I leave the club Art is getting into his car. When I arrive home I listen again to the tape I've made for him, wondering what I should do with it.

I finally decide to send the tape of songs with a note. As I sit down I feel a pull, a physical tug in my gut, telling me to pick up the pen and write to him.

I ask myself if I have ever experienced anything quite like this before, this compulsion to reach out to a person I have not met but identify with so strongly that I have to act. Thinking about it, I realize nothing quite like this has happened, but at the same time I recognize my need to reach out to Art as part of the new sense of myself that I am just barely beginning to allow to surface. Perhaps it was being with my family for the first time in several months and going to Peepaw's—my beloved grandfather's—funeral, the first funeral since Rod's. Or perhaps it is all the thinking about Rod—and crying—I've been doing. I can't put my finger on it completely, but I know that during the week back in Texas, I began paying attention to some memories I had long ago shunted to the back of my mind.

Around the age of seven or eight, as I listened to conversations taking place around me, I would know what someone was going to say before they said it. I would know where they had been that day or what they had done before they revealed it in their next comment. Sometimes I would get a physical feeling of good or bad news that was coming. I would find my stomach hurting when bad news was coming or feel unusually happy, even cry, when something good was going to happen. When I realized that other kids my age didn't have the same experiences, I began to push away the premonitions, wondering if it was "wrong" to know things, if maybe I was a little crazy.

Now, I realize, that intuitive part of me is awakening. Perhaps reaching out to another soul in pain will somehow ease my own pain, bring Rod closer in some way. I don't know, but this time I don't fight my instinct. Rather, I listen to it, deciding to trust myself for once. As I start writing the letter, the words flow easily.

Dear Art,

You don't know me personally or I you but I have grieved with you over your wife and two sons.

I can't imagine the pain you feel. There are no words to describe it or words to say. I understand and have been through some pain myself. I had a brother who committed suicide—I got the call and had to tell my family. I've been through a divorce and have had a lot of loss. It is so hard—some days are harder than others. You must know that.

My heart has broken for you. I remember the deep aloneness I felt and emptiness. No matter how strong I tried to be, the pain was great. I have felt that for you. I asked God to give me some of your pain to bear so you could have some easier days in your healing.

I have made this tape of songs for you to cry to, to smile to, to relate to . . . whatever. Music really helped me and still does . . . maybe it will help you— maybe not. I hope you enjoy it anyway for whatever purpose.

There is no reason for you to respond. I just want to reach out to you to support you and let you know you are being thought of. I saw you the other day at the Aspen Club—I'm always listening to music.

Take care —A Friend

My name doesn't seem important at the time. I am returning home to Texas in ten days, and we will never meet. He doesn't need my name, but my shared experience may help.

I take the letter and tape to the head postmaster at the small post office, nervous to tell this big, burly man with a graying beard and mustache what I am doing.

"I want to mail this to the man who lost his family in Glenwood Canyon," I say.

His demeanor softens, his eyes moisten, and he says, "Well, I know who that is. We've been getting a lot of mail for him."

"I don't have his address. Can you help me with that?"

"Well, by law, I can't give you his address. But . . . if you put his name, P.O. box with a question mark, Aspen, CO 81612, with your return address, I can get it to him," he explains. There is a line waiting to be helped. I feel their impatience.

I haven't planned on putting my return address, but it is the only way, in case of bombs, so I do. "Thanks for your help," I say as I hand him the finished product. I am almost afraid to let go of it.

"Sure," he says. There is a pause, then, "It's a horrible thing—what happened to him."

"It is. I think that's why I'm sending this," I say. He smiles, this time in his eyes. Despite the hurried people around me, time slows down. I walk slowly while people pass me, unintentionally bumping my shoulders. I walk to the newspaper stand as a diversion. My heart is both heavy and light. I sit down in a coffee shop and immerse myself in the news.

I'm making a quick round-trip to Florida in a few days, and I also need to begin packing to move back home to Texas. My thoughts turn to other things besides the letter. It is mailed and on its way. It has been an emotional process, and I have had doubts about sending it. It feels a little silly since I am a stranger.

When I come back from Florida, a week after I mail the letter, I stop by the post office and find a letter in my box addressed to "A Friend." I begin to shake as I look at it. Myriad emotions go through me. Mostly, I am disarmed. Why did he write me back? What does he have to say to me?

I prayed for him while I was out of town, and at times I feel the pain of his loss in my own body, although I wonder if I am making it up. I feel connected to this man but know he has no idea who I am. Holding the unopened letter, I don't know what to do. If I am honest with myself, I want nothing to do with his pain. The depth of it and amount of it seem overwhelming. At the same time, something powerful is drawing me toward him. Inside I know that something is going to happen. I don't know if I am ready for it, or exactly what it is, but I know in my gut that my life will change from it. My heart races as I open the sealed envelope to see what he has written. I sit down and lean against the wall of the post office. Once again people are passing by me with their busy lives. For me, time stops as I touch the paper and decipher his handwriting.

Dear Friend—
    Your note was so sensitive and caring that I want to reach out to you. If you're still experiencing loneliness of

your own, please let me know who you are—at the club, by phone, by mail. We have things to offer to each other. Let's not miss the opportunity to become friends.

I'm enjoying the music. Thanks for sharing a piece of yourself with me.

Art

A Leap of Faith

O THIS DAY I'M NOT SURE WHAT I WAS EXPECTING, OR HOP-
ing, would come of this. I've just lost my wife of twelve years,
and I've lost my beloved boys. The hole in me is so wide and
deep that it may take the rest of my life to fill it back up. And
I doubt that I have much capacity to feel something for someone else, at least not yet. But there is a part of me, secret, un-
observed, that is quietly beginning to search for someone to
love again. My spirit needs intimacy, although the rest of me
has never been particularly good at it. There are norms that
suggest that I wait a period of time before becoming involved
with another woman. But this isn't about anyone else; it's
about me, it's about doing whatever I can to become alive
again. So I guess the truth about writing back is, I do need
someone in my life, and a woman who can write that sort of
letter might just possibly be that someone. My faith in the
universe has been badly shaken, but I'm going to have to
keep on trusting in it. I really have nowhere else to go. And,

1

as implausible as it may seem, many of the songs on that tape were favorites of Kathy's. The woman who made the tape could not have known that.

Crazy?

I read the letter four times before I scoot myself up from the wall slowly, put the letter safely in my backpack, and walk across town to meet a friend for lunch. I keep the letter to myself and try to figure out why the idea of calling this man, of meeting him, scares me so much. It feels big to me. I am comfortable with pain. I know I can have an honest conversation with him and be present with his experience. That isn't what is scaring me. This man is obviously much older than me; he has just lost his family and is in a terrible place. At the end of the letter, he has left me his phone numbers. I don't call him that day or even the next.

"Have you ever called that man?" Kat is helping me box the last of my things to mail home. "You need to at least phone him," she says after I shake my head, my eyes turned down.

"I know. I am. Today." I continue to pack up and load boxes to take to the same post office where I received his letter. I am being a coward. I look around the room. It seems empty. I go over to the big windows and stare. I have no idea what I am doing in my life.

Kat leaves for a hike and I pull the letter out to read again. I take a deep breath, practice my normal tone of voice, and pick up the phone. I try his home first and there is an answering machine. I try the work number and am transferred through. While I am on hold I can feel my palms moistening. I curse myself as I hear a click. I want to hang up.

"This is Art Daily."

"Hi . . . this is A Friend. My name is Allison." I am talking way too fast.

There is a pause, and I hold my breath once again. I'm back in middle school, calling my crush Chris Kern. "Is this an okay time?"

"Yes. I'm sorry. I'm so glad you called. I wondered if you would." The sound of his voice is kind. All of a sudden I am at ease.

"Well, I've been nervous. I didn't know if I should. It felt funny."

"I know. But I really liked your letter, and I appreciate what you said. It's amazing because I get so many letters every day, and I decided to just pick yours up and read it. Most go into a basket until I feel up to reading them. I try to read a few every day. It's pretty overwhelming."

"I can't imagine." I realize the man wants to talk. "I am so sorry for what happened. I know those words don't help.

They don't touch it, but I am just so, so sorry for what has happened to you. I can't put it any other way."

"I am, too." His sadness is so transparent. "Every day I wake up wishing it were just a nightmare. To live it is almost unbearable. If it weren't for my daughter, Piper—she's twenty-four—from my first marriage, I don't know how I'd do it."

"There were days when I wondered if my mom would make it. Losing a child must be the worst kind of pain possible. I don't have kids, so I don't know that kind of love. Just watching my mom deal with my brother's suicide, I thought she might go crazy."

"You do feel like you're crazy a lot of the time." He hesitates. "I want to know about you. Do you mind?"

"No . . . I'm twenty-eight. I've been here about five months, just working and taking a break from the real world. I'm leaving in a few days to move back to Texas. I have a job waiting in Dallas." Talking with him seems comfortable.

"What brought you here?" he asks.

"Well, our family used to come to Snowmass in the summers. My dad was the guest tennis pro at the Snowmass Club. He's the University of Texas men's tennis coach now. Anyway, my brother committed suicide two months before I got married four years ago. That was the beginning of the end for me. I fell apart and the marriage did, too. I finally began looking at it with some help from a counselor. Six months ago I decided it was time for a little vacation from the pain and bad memories. My roommate and I loaded up a car and drove to Aspen."

"How do you like it here?"

"Well, I don't enjoy all the cold weather, but I love the people. Summer is actually my favorite time here." I pause. "It's been a good time for me to relook at my life. I've done a lot of that. Tell me about you."

"I'm a lawyer. I'm fifty-four. I'm a man who has lived a lot of his life for his family. I guess I'm trying to figure out who I am now." I can feel the questioning, the confusion.

I like the sound of his voice, the way he says things. I slowly pace in front of the big windows in my living room.

"Will you tell me about them, your family?" I want to know about them, and I know he needs to talk about them.

"It's funny how most people avoid the subject with me because they don't want to upset me."

"It's what I wanted when Rod died. Even my family didn't speak his name that often for a while. And yet everything in me wanted to scream, 'I miss him. So do you. Let's talk about it.' "

I hear relief in his voice, "Exactly. The only people who are open about it are the children. Shea and Tanner's friends are the ones who will talk about them. I need to talk about them." He's crying.

"I understand." We are silent for a while. I decide not to fill it but to let it stand on its own, emphasizing the pain we both know.

We continue talking about our lives and our pain for a long time. I am so at ease.

"Allison, would you consider having dinner with me before you leave?"

"I leave on Friday, and I have work or plans every night." I'm caught off guard. Talking on the phone is safe.

There is a pause. I don't think either of us knows where to go with it.

Art speaks first. "I have plans on Thursday. I'll break my plans if you'll change yours. How about it? I've enjoyed this and would love to talk more." It is very appealing. His voice is so kind.

"Okay. I'm supposed to go to the monastery with my friend Nancy. I think she'll understand. Where should we meet?" I lean against the glass pane and feel the heat of the sun against my body. How did this happen?

"The Silver City Grille. Do you know where it is?" He seems to smile over the phone. I smile back.

"Yes . . . say six thirty?" I am excited.

"Great. What do you look like? I'm five foot eleven and have gray hair."

"I know. I saw you briefly at the Aspen Club. I'm blonde, five foot eight, and have blue eyes."

"I'll see you then. By the way, thanks."

"Sure, see you then. I'm looking forward to it." I am.

I hang up the phone in a daze. I sit against the window and feel my back getting hot. I relive the conversation. I am surprised by him. I like his voice, its cadence and tone. I

feel I have known him a long time. My insides are churning—
it is by far the most interesting first conversation I have ever
had with a man. I am alarmed by my physical reaction to his
voice and our talk. The intimacy, the maturity, is attractive.
I'm not sure if that is okay considering he is in no way offer-
ing anything other than friendship.

"WOW!" I scream loudly. Kat is going to die over this. I
wish she were here for a girlfriend talk. I push against the
glass to boost myself up. Life is still in slow motion. It rarely
is with me. I walk into my room to dress for work, smiling.

Anticipation

ON THURSDAY THE WEATHER IS FINALLY TURNING WARM enough for spring bike riding, and around noon I change into biking gear, grab the road bike that leans year-round against the wall of my office, and head up Independence Pass for an hour or so to clear out my head and heart. The magnificent pass isn't open to auto traffic yet, and it's a perfect time to ride up there. Just as I'm clearing the valley floor and starting to climb, a car pulls up behind me and parks on the side of the road. As I stop pedaling and look back, a young woman jumps out of the car and trots up the road to me. "You're Art," she says. "I was just leaving my house at the bottom of the pass when I saw you ride by, so I thought I'd catch up with you and say hello. I'm Allison, your dinner date for the evening." I just sit there looking at her, not sure what to say. This girl is great. She just goes with her instincts and lets the chips fall all over the place. She seems really alive. I can almost touch her vitality, her spirit. And she's nice looking— blue eyes and blonde hair under a baseball cap, big floppy sweatshirt that hides the rest of her. I find my tongue and say, "Hi there, it's nice to see you in person. I'm just taking a run through the beauty of the day. I wish you had a bike, you could join me." Allison says, "I haven't done much riding, but I'd like to learn. Please go on. I didn't mean to interrupt your ride. I just wanted to see you up close." She gets back in her car, U-turns, and heads back down the road. I slowly climb back on my bike and begin riding the steep lower sections of the pass, a soft glow radiating through me. This girl has touched me. There's a subtle feeling of excitement, of expectation. A small smile creeps onto my face. And yet a part of me is keeping a firm lid on my emotions. I can't afford to let the dogs run. My passions are so raw, so exposed, and are such strangers to me. They can't take any more wounds. Still and again, the rest of the ride is filled with a quiet wonder.

I arrive at the Silver City Grille ahead of her, toss my jacket on a chair at an empty table, and walk across the room to talk with a boy named Nicki and his parents. Nicki had driven to Vail with us that day, watching movies in the rear seat with Tanner and Shea, and had played on Shea's Mites team. His parents drove over in another car, and he returned with them. Thank God he wasn't with us. Nicki is a sweet and thoughtful young man, and he's glad to see me. They check in on how I'm doing, and we chat for a few minutes until Allison walks in the door.

Speaking from the Heart

The Grille is a small dive crowded with little tables that are covered with colorful plastic cloths. I have never been in here but I like the feeling. It's a casual locals' joint. One of the waiters has dreadlocks and I wonder to myself how long it took to grow them. I feel overdressed in my "Texas attire," including makeup.

I see Art right away talking to a family in the corner. I take the opportunity to study him. He looks up, makes eye contact with me, and smiles. His eyes are arresting, even in their tenderness. I stay back in order to let him finish the conversation and try not to be too obvious in my staring. All I can think is, "Oh God!" He is so handsome and charming even in the way he carries himself. I am attracted to him on a very superficial level. I love his smile as he comes to bring me to his table.

"Hi, come on over." The man and woman he was talking with are wondering who I am. "Have you ever eaten here?" Art seems oblivious to the stares from around us.

"No, I haven't. It's a fun place." I am uncomfortable being looked over. I try to think of other things. "What's good to eat?"

Once we order and put our menus down, I play nervously with my hair. Art turns his chair in a way that those around can't see him as well. I do the same. He is trying to put me at ease and his effort alone makes me feel better. We talk on the surface about our lives. I study his face and eyes while he talks. I find myself centered on him; those around are a blur. When the waiter brings our food, I am taken aback that someone else is in the room. As Art and I eat and talk more personally, I realize I can't take my eyes off him.

"Allison, tell me about your brother," Art asks quietly as he leans in closer.

"I feel like we should talk about your family. I want to know all about them," I say. Ears spring up. The waiter comes back to refill our water. He pours in slow motion and we watch, waiting to finish the conversation. The ice cracks against the glass. His timing isn't great. Finally he leaves and we move closer together. I am so not okay with my reaction to this man.

"We'll get to them, I promise. I think of them so much, I'd like to hear about you first," he says, reaching out to touch my hand. His hand stays on mine after he squeezes it and I feel my body respond.

The only way I can describe the conversation is to say that it is a sharing of pain. I tell him about Rod, the loss in my heart, and the effect on my family. We talk of suicide and what it does to the parents of the victim. There is no judgment, only caring. He introduces me to Kathy, Shea, and Tanner through his words and descriptions of them. He talks of his time with Ram Dass, and he discusses a grief counselor he is seeing. He shares the experiences he is having in learning to face his loss head on and not run from it. He also tells me about the town of Aspen and how loving and supportive the people are to him.

All of the pain I had asked God to give me for him lies resting in my heart. As he talks of Tanner and Shea with tears streaming down his face, I want to give up my own life just for him to have them back in his arms.

As the restaurant clears and our waiter asks us if we want more decaf for the fifth time, Art smiles and asks me to come to his home. He wants me to see pictures of his family. I hesitate, not sure where this is heading and not sure if I can handle the pain. As we walk out to my car and I get in, we are both aware I haven't given him an answer. I have masterfully changed the subject, but he doesn't want to play that game.

"I'd really like you to come over," he says, touching my hair for a brief second.

I am a pile of melted ice cream. "Okay." He gives me directions.

Entering his driveway, I want to turn around and leave. The pulling, the calling inside, telling me, "This means something. This is big, Allison," is screaming into my ear. My whole life I have run, yet as I turn off my car engine I am aware I am walking toward it. I am afraid and yet not afraid at all. I knock on Art's front door. I feel liberated as I walk in. A different voice enters, a new one.

The house is older, comfortable and homey. There is evidence of his family everywhere. The walls are covered with art projects from school; there are toys in the corner. More than that, there is the feeling of their presence. My skin tingles. I don't feel Art and I are alone at all.

Art starts with Kathy, as he hands me her picture. I sit down so I can look carefully. He talks of her incredible strength. He tells me how she loved to help people and had been very involved in Temenos, a personal growth–type seminar; how she committed herself to seeing others make positive changes, like stopping an alcoholic from drinking himself to death. He is open and gentle about her and explains that while they had come to a good place in their marriage before her death, like any marriage it had had its ups and downs. I can feel the admiration for his wife and his deep respect for who she was as a mother to their boys.

"She looks serious," I say, pierced by her eyes. "Was she?"

"She was a no-nonsense woman. You always knew where you stood with her. So much that she did, though, was to help others. Even if they didn't want helping," Art says with a chuckle.

"Did she have a lot of friends?"

"She had a few close ones. She was a tough customer

and sometimes she was misunderstood. But she was very tight with a few women who were pretty solid themselves."

Tanner's soulful eyes look into me. I am drawn into him at once. "He looks sensitive," I say.

"Yeah, he was. He felt everything deeply." I can hear the catch in his voice. "He was the kind of boy who made sure everyone felt included and wanted."

I look again at Tanner, the silence palpable. "Our neighbor, Missy, was four years younger. She worshipped Tanner. He taught her how to ride her first bike without training wheels. He spent a whole afternoon working with her. When she was in kindergarten he rode the bus with her and picked her up from her classroom every day." I can tell Art feels he had much more to learn from his son.

Art picks up the last photo he has chosen to show me and tears stream down his face. He has a hard time releasing the photo for me to look at. An angelic face stares at me, eyes flashing joyfully. This is his soul mate. It isn't that he loves him more than Tanner; it is that there is a special connection. Shea drew something out in him that had never been touched before. "He was just a part of me in a way that nothing else has ever been. I would wake up in the morning and see him lying next to me . . . and I felt totally complete."

The love that Shea and Tanner shared together, and passed on to Art, was a gift in itself. It filled Art up in a way that nothing else could. Now it is gone. As we sit in silence on the couch, all three faces staring at us with very different expressions, I know he is wondering how he will survive without them.

We sit back on the couch and listen to music, talking until late. I am leaving for Denver the next day and then on to Texas. We talk about this and I wonder how it can be that I have met this man, discovered his world, the night before my life is heading in a very different direction. There is no future for me in Aspen, no reason for me to stay. We continue to share pieces of our lives until I begin to fall asleep. He asks for my address and phone number in Texas. I will leave his house knowing his family, and him, very well.

As we stand in the doorway, my knees are wobbly with his closeness. I am melting. Art leans over, puts his fingers under my chin and looks at me before he gently, softly, kisses me. When I make it into bed later I wonder how my legs carried me from the doorway to the car.

On my way to Denver the next day, I drop off three roses at his door with a note: "Thank you for letting me meet Kathy, Shea, and Tanner. Love, Allison."

The Fearless One

What an intimate evening. There is a purity in this woman that I haven't known. She's shy and warm and yet shining with inner strength. And there's more than a touch of spice. I find myself describing my deepest feelings to her, my fragile hopes, my ever-present fears. She wants to know the hard things, so I talk about the accident and I tell her about the ones I lost and how they were my life. She tells me of the death of her brother Rod and its devastating effect on herself and her family. We speak of happier things, too, and we speak the truth, and as the evening passes, we grow increasingly comfortable with each other. If the lateness of the hour hadn't caught up with us, I think we might have talked for days and told each other everything there was to tell. By nature, I am not all that talkative, particularly about personal matters, but somehow the rules have changed tonight. Allison has a way of focusing her gaze on me when I'm speaking, and even when I'm not, that is occasionally so intense that I'm not sure what to do with myself. She is walking right into my pain, my life, without judgment and without fear. I've never met anyone like this, and I am attracted to her on many levels. And for the first time since the accident, I find myself fully present. Kathy and Shea and Tanner are with me, but it is as if they are part of the now, rather than the past, and I feel very alive.

The next day she is gone. I'm left with three sweet flowers and the memory of an evening that touched me everywhere. She has a job waiting for her in Dallas and no plans to return to the mountains. I can tell that she really enjoyed being with me, but that doesn't mean she wants to change her life around so she can see me again. What am I going to do about all this? Should I let it ride? My plate is overflowing in every direction, I can't seem to bring much of anything under control, and I doubt that I'm big enough or tough enough to try to bring a strong young Texas lady into my life as well. Hell, I'm not sure I could have handled her in the best of times. Under the circumstances, it probably wouldn't be fair to her either. On the other hand, I suppose I could just wander over to the phone and check to see that she got home safely. As my mom used to say to me, "Nothing ventured, nothing gained." I don't think I ever really understood what she meant before, but it sure seems to fit this one. Oh man, what's the right thing to do here, for all of us?

I wish I had a way to check in with Kathy and the boys. Above all things, I don't want to do anything to dishonor our love for each other, our trust in one another. My devotion to them is as pure and as absolute as anything I have ever experienced in this life, and it will always be so. I miss them and long for them in every waking moment and probably in most of my dreams. And yet if an empty space of this dimension suddenly appeared in a forest, I know that nature would fill it with as much lushness and beauty as it could. It's the immutable way of our universe when vacuums occur. The human heart seems a lot like that forest. Shatterings are meant to be mended, holes to be refilled. And I believe that God, who created the extraordinary hearts of all beings, intended that they always be full, and that when they are filled with sorrow, an equal measure of joy must be brought forth in order to restore the essential balance of things. This is the magic of hope, the searing heat and glow of our eternal spirit.

Kathy, dear Kathy. It actually feels more like you are checking in with me than me with you, that you are working to keep me open, that you are driving strong winds beneath me, that you have somehow brought Allison into my life. I don't know these things to be true, but then again maybe I do. I search my heart for what is right, for what you would say to me, and somehow I sense your encouragement in seeking new love and companionship. And all lines of energy appear to meet in Allison. Tanner and Shea? That's easy. They're all over this. I can feel their own sorrow lifting, the veil of snows that has descended upon them starting to thaw. They want only happiness for their dad, and they want to be close to me always. They, too, have had a part in choosing Allison, and they are going to stay the course to see that it happens. For them, she is to be the force that keeps our love alive and fully present.

Piper has been living with me since the accident, and

another young woman has also moved into the house. Pandora was Shea's nanny and is now engaged to be married, but she is one of the most loving people I've ever known and she simply decides that I need her and that she is going to help take care of me for a while. So the house that has lost so much of its aliveness is never empty. Piper and Pandora were very close to the boys and Kathy, and we talk endlessly about them, about where they are now, and I try to describe who I am without them. Falling asleep at night and waking in the morning to the stark truth of another day are still the hard times. I've bought a new sound system for the bedroom; it's part of the changing, shifting, moving, the battle to stay open, to embrace life as it is. We crank it up, sometimes sitting against the dresser with headphones on, and immerse ourselves in Gregorian chants, or Enya, or the rolling thunder and mystical rain of a great storm, and they hold me when I fall apart and cry so desperately that I can't breathe, curled up on the rug like a child. My heart and my soul are torn so badly. I could not do this alone.

And now I talk with Piper, and sometimes with Pandora, about the first letter I received from Allison and about my evening with her, and I tell them how confused I am about how it all fits together. Is there a moral issue here, an ethical question? Or is the universe just evening the playing field, saying, "There have been dark hours here, terrible pain and loss, and it is right and fair that there be an opportunity for equal or greater joy." In which case the choice is truly mine, and mine alone. Piper's take is, "Dad, she sounds like a very cool girl, I think you ought to go for it." I'm scared that I may try and fail, that I may end up in an even bleaker hole, but the high and secret place in me that cherishes life in all its great sweep and range answers, "God save all here, let's get on with it."

I call Allison at her parents' home in Austin, and I tell her how much I liked being with her and that I want to see her again. To my delight and relief, she says that she feels the same way, and she makes arrangements to fly back to Aspen for a long weekend.

We spend most of our days outdoors, and as this time of soft colors and long glowing silences flows around and beneath us, we begin to acknowledge the power of our feelings for each other. We don't know where to go with it or even how to talk about it very well, but we feel it and we see it in each other's eyes.

"You're an amazing person, Allison. I've never talked this much in my life." We're at dinner in a quiet restaurant.

"No, I'm not actually. I'm really just an insecure woman who likes to caretake and talk about it." She takes a sip of her wine and I see her eyes change. After her second sip, I see the tears forming.

"What's wrong?" I reach out and touch her across the small table.

The candle on our table flickers and then settles again. People walk by being shown to their table. My eyes never leave hers.

"I'm not sure. Maybe I'm just overwhelmed. I really like

you. I can't find anything wrong with you and believe me I can find something wrong with any man on a first date."

"This is a third date. No, fourth."

"It's not funny. I think you are such a special person and while I am a caretaker, what I feel for you isn't really about that."

"Maybe that's because I don't want you to take care of me," I say, squeezing her hand in reassurance. I love watching her eyes change with her moods. "I'm in a lot of pain, Allison, but it's my own pain. If we continue to see one another, you'll have to let me cry and rage and do what I need to. You can be there, but you can't rescue me."

"Art, I've been wondering, what's going through your mind about getting involved with me so soon after losing your family?"

This woman is sure direct. I think of how to answer this with sensitivity to all involved, myself included. "Yeah, in a way I feel guilty that I'm beginning to have strong feelings for you so soon. In my heart I battle with holding Kathy and the boys close—and yet I know they are gone." It's the first time I have said this out loud and it's a relief to say it.

"What do you think Kathy would say about me, us?" Allison asks. I almost drop my glass.

"Well, first of all, I think she'd like you. Just for asking that, she'd like you. A lot." I pause, really picturing Kathy and her reaction to my being involved with Allison. "I think one part of her would be mad at me and another part of her would be proud that I am beginning to rejoin the human race."

"What about the boys? What would they think?"

"I think they'd be thrilled. Kids' hearts are so pure, so clean. They would know that I need to find peace and joy since their mom—and they—are dead." Tears fill my eyes and a lump sticks in my throat. I look down and see Allison's hand covering mine. A part of me had left for a second, gone to a place in my heart that wants nothing more than to be with them. I don't want to die; I just want them home with me.

"Thanks for being honest. That wasn't easy. It sounds weird, but having all that out in the open makes it easier for me to allow myself to care about you even deeper. I had been thinking that if I were Kathy I'd be really angry at you. I can't help but feel protective, as a woman. And yet here I am, 'the other woman.' I just want to stay open about all of this."

I look at her and like her more than ever. We eat in silence for a while. Then I ask Allison to tell me more about Rod. As she begins to talk about him I can see how fresh her wounds and memories still are. My own recent experience has opened a door for her, and the pain and anguish pour out.

"A part of me turned off when Rod died," she says. "The shock and horror of his death, the terrible hole that it left in me, the anger and the sadness, have never really gone away. It sometimes feels like I'm covered with an extra layer of skin.

"You know, Art, this is the first time that I've ever wanted someone to understand how I feel about Rod, to know everything about him. Somehow it doesn't feel like you're judging me or trying to protect me. It's more like I'm receiving a gift of calmness in my storm of grief. I finally want to let someone in. I've actually written a short memoir about Rod and his death. I called it 'Looking for Rod.' I'd like you to read it sometime."

It's a long and emotional evening for both of us, and neither of us wants it to end. But it is clear that it will not be our last evening together—so perhaps the strongest emotion is hope.

As Allison prepares to fly back to Texas, she tells me that she has plans to hike into the Grand Canyon with friends, and she promises to call me when she returns home again.

Looking for Rod

I wake up in a sweat. I sit up and look around. It's so dark. Where am I? I calm myself down, reminding myself I'm at home. Rod was right here, I think to myself. He was so close. What was he saying? He was trying to tell me something, but I can't find it in the haze of my mind. My heart is beating so fast it feels as if it is going to jump out of my chest. I lie down and close my eyes again, hoping he'll return, but it doesn't help. Instead I begin feeling the loss all over again. It's almost two months since he died and yet it feels like yesterday. I wonder how deep this pit in the bottom of my stomach will go. Is there a time limit on grief? I try to go back to sleep. I am in his old bedroom in the house we grew up in, sleeping in the bed he used for years. The soft mattress envelops me as I hold on to a pillow for comfort.

I surrender to the memories, the guilt, the hollowness I feel. I hear our dog, Penny, move around near the stairs and I wonder if she feels the sadness as well. All of a sudden the need for noise, for distraction is primal. My body wants to escape the rising emotions that are coming in waves. I pull the pillow over my head and breathe in his scent. I hold my breath for longer periods of time, hoping I will feel him again. Can his smell bring him closer? It is heaviest here, inside this pillow that was always his. As I inhale this lingering part of him, I am strangely comforted.

"Rod, save me! He's going to get me!" I run into Rod's room—barge, rather—and slam the door behind me. I am behind him, hiding from my other brother, Doug, who is chasing me. Rod has heard our distant screams and slamming doors and is prepared for the inevitable bothering.

"I got you. Don't even dare to hide behind Rod. You're dead meat." Doug is coming at me. Rod's my only protection.

"Hey! Both of you knock it off." Rod has been peacefully drawing cartoon characters, his favorite hobby, before we shatter his creativity. Solitude and the creatures he invents are his best friends. "Doug, leave her alone."

I am shaking behind Rod, partly out of fear, partly for drama. "Yeah, Doug, leave me alone."

"She was snooping in my desk, reading my letters. They're private." Doug is beyond anger, justly. He is discovering girls and the love letters reveal his secrets.

Rod talks to me slowly and calmly while still holding his arms out to protect me. "Did you do that?"

"Yeah, but I didn't read anything bad," I say, as if that justifies the sneaking.

"Only because you didn't find the good ones." Doug is hoping Rod will release me. I am eight and Rod is babysitting me. His eyes meet mine.

"I would hand you over to the wolf if I wasn't in charge of your well-being. That was a rotten thing to do. Stay away from his stuff. Got it?" Rod sends Doug a warning with his eyes that the fight is over.

"Got it," I say, sending a thankful glance. I am just learning about boys, especially watching my own brothers as they go through changes. Their bodies are filling out and their voices deepening. Pimple medicine and cologne cover the bathroom counter we all three share. Moods are varied and they no longer will wrestle and play with me the way they used to. I am more of a nuisance. My rebellion, my curiosity as to what is happening becomes snooping as I look for clues as to where my "old brothers" have gone—to find out who these "new ones" are.

Rod, eight years my senior, is attractive in a soft, kind way. His darkening blond hair comes just over his glasses and face and helps to mask a gentle young man and gifted artist who draws for grassroots magazines and comic books. While his art shows promise, he uses it more as a retreat from the world around him. There is nothing distinctive about his build or features, and because of that he has been easily overlooked most of his life. He is a gift waiting to be opened. His green eyes are warm, willing to see the goodness in anyone. Though he has strong athletic abilities, he has chosen to ignore them, maybe even to rebel from the

family that worships them. Instead, he retreats to his room
for hours at a time alone with his pencil and paper and his
loud rock music. From the beginning I have understood and
related to Rod's confusion with the world and some of the
hard things that happen in it.

Doug, the golden child of our family, is an all-American
blond athlete who excels at all sports and school. He walks
with confidence, knowing he can do whatever he sets out to
do. He's four years older than me and is a magnet to others.
I am in love with him at times, admiring the ease with which
he moves through life. I look up to him and want to be as popular as he is. While Doug is my mentor, Rod is my soul mate.

Back in Rod's old bed I see it is getting lighter and my mind
smiles as I think of Rod as my watchdog. I rub my palms in
circles against the cool sheets and, in the darkness that
fades right before morning light breaks through, I stare at a
picture he drew years ago—I'm unsure when—that is hanging on the stark white wall. It is a black and white abstract.
My mind has made it into a bullfighter holding his cape
close by his side as a bull slides by. The fighter is brushing
death, daring it to beat him. He stands with both confidence
in his abilities and in awe of this creature that has barely
nicked him with its horns. The bull has black fire protruding from its nostrils and fury in its eyes—hating this game
the man plays with him—knowing death is imminent. I want

to know what Rod was thinking when he drew it. When he died, I found I had thousands of questions I forgot to ask him. If indeed it is the picture that I see in my head, I think that Rod must have felt like fighter and bull all in one. He must have known his intelligence and artistic abilities could take him far in life and yet his heart was broken by the problems of the world—poverty, wars, starvation, cruelty. Burdened by the world's unfairness, he couldn't allow himself to celebrate and share his own gifts. Instead, depression surrounded him and took him away.

I breathe in his essence from the pillow on his bed again, wondering where his favorite tennis racquet disappeared to. A few days ago I saw a racquet in his old closet and wondered if it was his. While Doug and I grew up playing competitive tennis with our dad, Rod used his racquet as a makeshift guitar.

"What are you doing?" I am knocking vehemently on Rod's door to tell him it is time for dinner and to turn down the music.

Rod opens the door but continues to play his guitar/ tennis racquet and sing along. Everything about his body and his facial expressions shows me he thinks he is in the band right now. Finally the song ends and he becomes Rod again. "It's Jefferson Starship—they're hard core." His inclusion of me draws me to him—and his music—even more.

"They're okay. I like Alice Cooper more. Can I borrow your album on Friday night for the sleepover?"

"Yeah, if you take good care of it. Are you girls dressing up again?" he asks.

"Yeah." A few weeks ago some of my girlfriends and I had made up our faces with dark makeup and danced and pretended we were the Alice Cooper band, mouthing the words. We stood on the fireplace as our stage, using sticks from the yard as our microphones. Rod had walked in on our performance and smiled the smile that melts my heart.

"Mom says it's time to eat. Come on."

"One more song and I'll be down. Close the door," he says. Rod turns up the music again, picks up his tennis racquet and drifts back to his life as a world class guitarist. The words are in his body, expressing all the emotions he can't say out loud.

I know he is different, even then. I see him retreat within himself at times, how uncomfortable he feels relating to the rest of society and its expectations. Somehow his insecurity and discomfort give me the freedom to be closer to him, to protect him.

I walk back into his room and yell over the electric guitar blaring through the speakers, "I forgot to tell you . . . we're having liver tonight." I close his door again. He knows I'll go down to take the ketchup out of the refrigerator so we can survive the meal.

———

I look over to the window near the bed. Dawn is approaching. Today I would eat a hundred meals of liver if he would just be here to eat them with me. I'd even give up the ketchup and not hide some of my already chewed bites in my napkin. I'd even promise not to puke. Tears stream down my face as I wonder what kind of music he listens to wherever he is. I hope he has a tennis racquet there, too. I realize I'm talking out loud to this empty, dark space. I sit and listen and notice that there is a crackling in the darkness similar to being under water. I am trying to find him. I am looking everywhere—in my sleep and even in this darkness.

The yearning is a friend, the only ally that draws me closer to where he is. Thoughts of the phone call and mental pictures of his body and the gun enter and I feel like I may get sick. I go into the bathroom and lay my head against the cold tile.

"Rod. Are you here?" I'm home for lunch. It is two weeks before his death and I just turned twenty-four a week ago. When he asked me what I wanted that day I said, "To take a walk with you."

I taught tennis for three hours and I want to eat and change clothes before I walk with Rod as we had planned. I'm living at my parents' house until Duncan's and my wedding in just over two months. Rod's red truck is parked outside. I hope he hasn't come to cancel our date. "Rod, where are you?" I yell loudly. It's unusual for him to just stop by.

Rod comes toward me from Mom and Dad's room downstairs and his face is ashen. I put down the glass of ice water I have filled and look at his eyes. He diverts my look and picks up my glass and drinks from it. He's nervous, talking fast. "Hi. Well, why are you home? I'm just picking up something I left. Are we still walking today?"

"Yes. I came home to eat first." I pause, "Are you okay? You look weird."

"I'm fine. I don't want to meet you where we planned. I want to meet you by the high school. Okay?" He is fidgety and still won't look me in the eye. He walks toward the back door.

"Okay. I'll see you there at one thirty." I decide he's not in the mood to be pushed with questions.

"See you there. Bye." He is off at high speed. As I take out the lunch meat and bread, I wonder what has him upset. He can be so touchy, so sensitive I never know when to push. I never know how much to worry about him. He is so different, but I realize he has his own way of coping with his life. I open up the refrigerator and pull out the mayonnaise and mustard. If he came home to get something, why were his hands empty?

At twenty-four I'm still not sure who I am or exactly what I want out of life. If I had to pick an animal to best describe me, and I was being honest with myself, I'd have to choose a chameleon. I am able to blend in with my environment and to change my personality depending upon whom I am with. When I'm at work, I am just like the well-put-together social friends I have there. I can talk the way they do and be interested in all they are doing. When I'm at my Presbyterian church, I'm a solid Christian and know all the Bible verses and most of the right answers to the questions of faith. When I volunteer to make meals for the street people of Austin, and I look a woman in the eye and see her shame, her fear—I become her and I feel all of the hurt she carries. The amazing thing—maybe even sad—is that I think all the personalities are me. I can describe each of these people and their lives and what they believe. I just don't know who I am.

When we begin the walk around Town Lake, a running trail that encompasses a lake in the center of Austin, Rod is still tense. I see in his eyes that he needs me. At thirty-two, he's even more vulnerable to life than I am. His green eyes are glossed over, staring out and a little afraid. I find compassion taking over, begging me to hug my brother. We are like that. When he needs something, that the world—his world—is unable to give him, I'm able to pull it up and give it to him. It's as if the Universe has allowed me to be the keeper of his soul. It is too vulnerable to place anywhere else or it might break.

The conversation is forced in the beginning so I talk to him about my upcoming wedding and his role in it. "So, are you cool with being an usher? I'm going to let you escort Mom down the aisle."

"Sure."

"Earth to Rod . . . where are you?"

"I don't know. I'm just tired, I guess." He seems preoccupied, still fidgety.

"What's up, Rod? You've been acting strange today."

"Yeah, well. I feel weird, I guess." There are moments like this with him, times when I can look at his brain and almost see all the thoughts flying around. When he lets the feelings fly out, it is sudden, like a firecracker going off behind your back. He bursts out, "I just need to leave here. I just want to go. I'm not sure where. I was thinking maybe a Quaker community. They are peaceful there. . . . It's a place I think I could coexist with others."

"What's wrong with here? You just got your tree trimming service going and you're doing well. You have a lot of business." I had gone from mailbox to mailbox handing out flyers for his new enterprise.

"It's fine." His response sounds sort of hopeless.

"What is it, then?"

"I just want to be gone. I feel odd here somehow . . . like people are watching me, staring."

"Who is?" I pause, trying to make sense of this. A woman I know from the club runs by on the dirt path and I break my intensity with him and give her a big smile. The chameleon has changed her colors. I try to change back again. I feel like the color red with him now—the intensity, the love. "Rod, I told you I had seen that premarital counselor. He does all types of counseling. Do you want his name? I think it might be really good for you."

"No. I don't." He is sure. "I don't need to see anyone. I've been seeing that guy over at the men's center anyway." It's a New Age therapy center where Rod has attended groups and classes. It's a little airy-fairy for me but I try to listen to what he tells me about his sessions there. "A few of the people there think I might be gay. That's why I have a hard time having successful female relationships."

He has dropped the bomb. I walk a little slower, carefully thinking about my response. "Okay. How do you feel about that?"

We walk in silence. I am the color blue. A deep blue. I want to cover him with it, to wash away all of this uncertainty.

"I don't have any desire to sleep with another man." There is no anger, only frustration. What do I say to that? I wonder. "I was going to try one night, just try and see what it would be like. I feel like men have been staring at me, in the grocery, in the movie line, everywhere. I tried looking back at a guy one night at the movies."

I can't picture this at all. "What happened?"

"I went to the bathroom and cried. Then I almost threw up."

"Oh Rod." I touch his arm. Why can't I make myself be every good color, everything bright, and pour it into him? "I am so sorry."

Ten days later Duncan and I are finishing up teaching our tennis lessons, getting ready to leave for Midland, Texas, for a big wedding shower being given for us by two prominent families there, friends of his parents. My mom is going to take us to the airport after she finishes teaching her last day of tenth grade English for the year.

After my lesson I get in my car to go home and pack. I unlock the lever and push the button to release the convertible top. It's a pleasant May day. Not too hot yet. As I drive out of the club and turn onto the highway toward home, I take out my ponytail holder and shake my head, letting myself enjoy the feel of the wind in my hair. I turn up the radio and sing along, hoping to cover up the menacing feeling I have inside. I wonder if I'm nervous about meeting Duncan's friends and more of his family. As I pull into my parents' driveway, I remind myself not to forget the strappy black shoes that go with my favorite sundress.

When the phone rings, I am running up the stairs of my childhood home to pack. I jump the stairs two by two, timing myself in my head, a game I have played since I was a little girl. I make it in five seconds. As I get to the top of the staircase, I have an eerie feeling something is wrong. I look down at the phone I placed on the green shag carpet after an earlier call to Duncan and I realize I'm letting it ring and ring. I don't want to answer it. Something is wrong—I feel it in my bones. If I answer the phone I will know the answer. "Hello?"

"Who is this?" The woman's voice is frantic. "I need to know."

"I'm Allison Snyder. Who is this?"

"Are you sitting down? I need you to sit down." She is yelling. I can't think with her yelling.

"I am now. I'm sitting. What is it?" I am shaking. "What has happened?" I am screaming back at her.

"Your brother Rod has shot himself in the head. I'm in his house right now. I'm with him. He called me right before he did it, and I ran over here to try to stop him, but he'd already done it. There's a gun by his side. I don't know what to do. I'm sorry." There's a pause and I can't form words to talk to her. "There is blood everywhere. There's a note on his body for your family. It has this phone number on it."

"Are you sure? Are you sure he's dead? Are you sure?"

The woman proceeds to tell me the details. She is trying to stay calm but her voice gets louder and louder. "He took a gun to his head. His head isn't even a part of his body! There are brains everywhere—all over the walls. Ahhh. I can't believe what I'm seeing. This is so horrible! How do I clean it up? I am going to throw up again." She throws up and then comes back on. I am trying not to picture in my mind all she is telling me but I can't help it.

"How did you find him? How did you know?" I ask. I can't find the right questions.

"He called me. I walked in just after he left the message. He said he was going to do it but didn't want your family to be the ones to find him." She has gone in the other room to get away from the mess. Her voice is a little more calm, maybe from having someone to share this with. "I came as fast as I could. I'm sorry it wasn't in time. I had no idea. I'm so sorry for all of you." She begins to cry and I wonder how to comfort her. She and Rod took a public speaking class together. He mentioned her to me once—how kind she'd been.

I say to her, "I don't know what to do. What should I do first? Please don't apologize anymore." I can't think. My body is shaking. "You don't need to. I'm just so sorry that you are seeing all of this." What she did in trying to stop him, and then calling me, was very brave. I just want to get off the phone with her and try to think. She continues to repeat things and finally I say, "I need to call my mom. Are you okay?"

She assures me she is going to get help for herself. She has called the police to report the suicide. At the funeral she will introduce herself to me but in my shock and grief I'll forget her name. I'll never see her again.

As I hang up the phone, my first thought is, "How do I tell Mom and Dad?" I have chills all over my body. I want to cry, but when I think of what I must do now, I stop. I move into survival mode. It's as if another person comes in and takes over my physical body so I can manage. I call Duncan and leave a message at the club to come quickly. I try to call Doug, but he's left for the weekend. Then I pick up the phone to do the unthinkable.

"Westlake High School. May I help you?" the secretary says.

"Yes, I need to speak to Nancy Snyder. Can you please help? It's an emergency!" I know she's packing up her classroom for the summer holidays.

"Yes, hold on." Elevator music comes on. I think of what to say to her. She's my mom, my best friend, and yet in this moment she is Rod's mom.

"This is Nancy Snyder."

"Mom, I need you to come home right away," I say.

"I know, honey. I haven't forgotten I'm taking you to the airport."

"Mom, this is different. Come home *now*." I'm losing any sense of calmness.

"What's wrong, Allison? What has happened?" I can hear the panic creeping in.

"Just come home, Mom. I'll tell you then. Please hurry." I hang up, knowing I can't hold it together any longer with her.

How am I going to tell her once she gets home? I can't even go there in my mind, so I decide to find my dad. I think he's playing golf, so I give that a try.

"Barton Creek Golf, this is Paul." My heart feels relief. Paul and I dated for years and he's a close friend of our family. He's the director of golf, and I know he'll find my father.

"Paul, this is Allison." I begin to sob.

"What's wrong, Allison? Are you okay?" he says.

"Paul, I need you to do something for me. I'm so sorry. Rod has killed himself. I have to get my dad home so I can tell him. I need you to go get him. Don't tell my dad what's happened; just tell him there is a family emergency and to come home. Will you do that?" I waver between calmness, logic, and hysteria. The reality of what has just happened is all around me and yet I can't face it. Paul knows not to ask any questions.

"I will. I'm so sorry, Allison. I'm so sorry. I'll go get your dad myself and make sure he leaves right away," Paul says.

"Thank you, Paul. Bye." I hang up and pace the floor, knowing all I can do now is wait . . . wait for the first one to walk in the door so I can tell them. My body begins to shake.

Duncan walks into the house. I tell him the details, feeling sick. He holds me at first and then the next minute the thought of physical contact repulses me. I keep shaking out my arms as if I can shake away this horror. I don't want anyone near me. I want to go crazy and yet I know I have to hold it together. I can't figure out how I'm going to tell either of my parents what their eldest child has done. I can't believe that I'll never see him again.

My mom walks into the house, concern all over her face. I walk her back to her bedroom. Duncan waits in the kitchen for my dad. "Mom," I am trying to figure out how to do this. "Something bad has happened. I don't know how to tell you."

"What is it, Allison? Who has died?" She's already going crazy, and I'm scared to tell her who.

"Rod. He shot himself in the head. He's dead."

"NO! NO!" Her screams are terrible. I try to hold her, to help, but there is nothing I can do. She needs to do this. Why can't I fall apart, break down? I feel detached and unable to believe that this is really happening.

She is pulling her hair. She is possessed by anguish. She goes to her dresser and pulls out a letter Rod had written to her a week before. The letter asks her to let go of him, to pray for him. He has been involved with an alternative New Age therapy and he's trying to find an answer to his failed relationships. The letter might easily be interpreted to blame her and she is already taking on the responsibility for his suicide. I can't make sense of the letter and I can't get the images out of my mind of him dead. I try to tell her it's not her fault. There is no point in even trying. She's going there because she loves him with all her heart. He's her first born. He's also her troubled one. She has a beautiful connection with him and he's the one she has spent most of her time worrying about. Her child is gone now, and by his own volition. The only person she can blame is herself.

We sit on the bed. She paces, screams, and pounds on anything she can find. Eventually she calms enough to simply cry, so I hold her. I think back on the memories of my oldest brother. I see a boy who plays his tennis racquet to the Band, Creedence Clearwater Revival, and Alice Cooper. He is for peace on this earth, living in harmony, and free choice. He's a man, a boy really, who sees the good in others and finds himself so disappointed when the bad comes out.

"Allison, I want to go! I need to see his body and know it is real. What if it isn't true? I'm going."

"NO! Mom, you can't. It's horrible. The woman who called said it's bad. I don't want you to see that. Wait here until Dad comes home. Just wait." There aren't words to describe that kind of time. I am numb. I will stay that way for more than a year.

My dad walks into the bedroom, and we tell him. I watch them fall apart together. Late afternoon sun hits a figurine on the dresser, reflecting a prism on the wall. I leave the room, knowing they need time to grieve their son alone. I don't know where to go.

Back in Rod's bed I hug his pillow. I feel the tears drying on my cheek, causing my skin to tighten from the salt. My breath catches and finally I sigh deeply, releasing my body from the final sobs. It's quiet again and the crackling sound of the air is back. The air conditioner flips on and the drumming sound comes through the vents. I realize that it doesn't matter what I knew or didn't know on that day. It doesn't change anything. I am not responsible, but I will live with guilt simply because I have been a witness to his pain, his questioning, for many years of his life. He confided in me as he traveled from commune to commune, job to job, searching for peace within himself and with others. I gave him my open mind in a society that was more closed; he shared with me his pain and I carried it in my palm for years. Sometimes my hand was wrapped around it; other times it was held carelessly. It was always with me. I couldn't have stopped him from buying that gun and pulling the trigger. He made that decision apart from me.

When he died, there were a lot of IOUs to him tacked to his wall. In his last note, he absolved all of those debts. It was his final gift.

Another Canyon

Shortly before Art and I meet, my buddy Laurie calls me
from Austin to tell me that two of her friends have a permit
to hike the Grand Canyon in May and there are two spots
open on the permit.

"Let's go. We've never done anything like this before.
Bob and Rebecca will be fun to go with," Laurie says. Bob
and Rebecca are married, both doctors. I know them casually. I like them and want to take a trip with Laurie—to whom
I have been close for almost five years—before I start the
new job in Dallas working for a man who buys and sells
companies. I'm not sure hiking the Grand Canyon is what
I had in mind. I haven't hiked much and I'm a little intimidated by the idea. Laurie and I talk awhile, and I decide to go
for it. The dates work perfectly with when I finish working in
Aspen, and I can do some warm-up hikes to get in shape.

I go to the Ute Mountaineer and buy myself some good
hiking boots. I wear them everywhere to break them in. I hike
up my favorite trails, alternating between hard and easy ones.

When the streets aren't covered with late spring snow, I get my thirdhand bike out and ride it to and from work at the Chart House. I know I'm not ready for the Grand Canyon, but I'm as ready as I'm going to be.

We leave for the trip just days after I return to Austin after the weekend with Art. I'm still reeling from the whole experience and I can't identify the emotions I have when thinking of him. He's handsome and mature in a way that older men can be. I sense he knows things that I don't yet know. It's something deeper that attracts me to him, though. He's raw from his brutal loss and it has left his emotions on the surface. Like the pendant he now wears around his neck, his pain is close to his heart.

I've grown tired of the games played in my past relationships. I'm tired of guessing. I yearn for honesty and openness in another as well as myself. I want a man who knows who he is and what he wants. I don't want him to depend on me but to let me be a part of his heart, his life. In that first short evening with Art, despite the horrible pain he's in and maybe even because of it, I saw glimpses of the qualities I've been looking for but have almost given up on finding. After our weekend together, I'm glad that Laurie and I have made plans for the hike—it will give me time to think.

Art calls me in Texas the night before we leave for the Grand Canyon. He's sending me a videotape of the memorial service to watch when I get back. I think it odd to have taped a memorial service, but Art explains that this one is different; he, Piper, and Kathy's closest friends had either talked or sung and had celebrated the three lives that were lost. A lot of people came. I can tell Art wants me to see it so that I can know his family even better. He also knows I'll learn more about the kind of man he is. We talk for a while about his grieving, his work, and my trip. I can tell that he enjoys me but doesn't need me to save him in any way. That in itself seems amazing. We agree to talk after I get home, though neither of us knows where the relationship is heading. I know I've met a man I respect and want to know better; he has given me new hope.

Laurie and I fly into Phoenix, rent a car, and drive toward the South Rim of the Canyon, where we'll meet up with Bob and Rebecca. I've been living in the mountains so the dry, sparse landscape seems barren. As we drive, the tall cacti and unusual brush surrounded by Mediterranean style houses grow on me. I feel a loneliness as we head toward the Canyon. A light shawl of heaviness is being draped over my shoulders. It isn't uncomfortable or unwelcome; rather it feels it has found its home. I wonder where it has come from—if it's in me or around me. As we drive through the desert I think more of my time with Art, of seeing the pictures of his family. I think of his sadness. I wonder if I am carrying his or my own.

"So you really think you are experiencing some of his pain . . . like he has less because of you?" Laurie says, part sarcasm, part curiosity.

"No. Not exactly." I pause. "I don't even know what I believe, really. I just know I can feel this pain that I'm sure has something to do with me but feels like it has more to do with someone else."

"Oh." She thinks a minute. "Well, what are you going to do about it?"

"Nothing," I reply. "I asked for it."

"Well, you could take it back, ya know?"

"Laurie, that's not the point. I care for this man."

"I know, but it seems a little dysfunctional to me. And you've just met him. How can you have such strong feelings?" she says, continually baffled by my intense emotions.

"I can't explain any of it, and wouldn't try, even to you. All I can tell you is that I met this man I've been praying for and had an instant connection to him. He's beautiful, Laurie." I pause, trying to find the right words to describe him. "He radiates, even in his pain. I've never felt totally surprised by a man like this. I see goodness in him, depth."

Laurie looks over with a dubious expression. "Just don't go off and marry him."

We laugh at that, her more than me, and pull off to the side of the road to stretch our legs.

I was born in Tucson, lived there till I was four. I remember one family we were close to and continued a close relationship with even after we moved to Texas because of my father's new job as the University of Texas men's tennis coach. Mary Kay was my mother's best friend and that never changed. One memory from my short time living in the desert was that of the love between my mother and Aunt Mary Kay. As all of us kids (my mom's and Aunt Mary Kay's) played and made up games, the two women would share coffee, laugh, and talk for endless hours. A little girl who admired her mom, I often gauged my own emotional stability by hers. The years in Tucson were happy ones.

I look over at Laurie in the car and smile, thinking of all of the times she has been there for me—especially during my divorce, now three years behind me. I recall the endless card games we played while I lived with her and her family. She has been a home base, a safe place, someone I can tell my deepest and darkest thoughts to. She opened up her house, her heart, her family to me during a time when my self-esteem was low and my heart heavy. She's rarely judged me; rather, she has questioned along with me. She listened to me and witnessed my pain during a time when others were trying to tell me what was right or wrong.

I first met Laurie when she came to the Austin Country Club and signed up for a private tennis lesson with me. I'd seen her and her husband around the club. I knew they'd just moved to Austin from California. During the first lesson we talked while picking up balls and found we had a lot of common interests. I was intimidated by her because my impression of her was that she had this fairy-tale life. She and her husband drove around in a monster Mercedes, had two cute kids, had just built a mansion in a new development—and she had a very expensive taste in clothes. When she asked me to go out to lunch later that day,

I almost swallowed my tongue. We decided to meet at T.G.I. Friday's at noon. Duncan laughed at me as I sat in our small office and panicked. "What am I going to talk to her about?"

"I don't know. What is it you girls talk about when you have lunch?"

"Those lunches are with girls I know. Laurie scares me."

"Why would she possibly scare you?" he said.

"I guess because she seems to have it all together. She has it all. I can't imagine that."

"Just be you, Allison. You are so much more than you think. Just tell her about yourself, and find out about her."

I stayed nervous all through lunch and asked her a million questions to avoid my own story. Laurie was kind and shy. I had mistaken the shyness for arrogance and as we talked I realized she had fears and inhibitions just the way I did.

I began giving her tennis lessons once or twice a week and we began doing more and more together. I learned that she had come from a middle-class family, but her lifestyle had changed after she married Dwight. Though they had plenty of money, her life and marriage held secrets and pain like the rest of the world. I told her about my family and Rod. We both opened our lives to one another and tested the waters, seeing if a friendship could hold up to seeing one another's warts. As time went on, we both realized that the parts we had initially feared the other would reject were actually the glue that held us together. In time she gave me a key to her house, the security code, and full access to her closet. I gave her my heart.

Our two favorite hobbies were shopping for clothes and playing spite and malice, a card game, while drinking wine at her kitchen table. We had a special deck of cards for our games that were a red and orange paisley design. We had bought them to take on a girls' trip to Mexico shortly after I had married Duncan. We went to a resort and did nothing but play cards, read books, sit in the sun, and eat when necessary. We played and read until all hours of the night. We came back rested and content, but the cards were pretty worn out.

I had been seeing a therapist named Tom a lot in those days before I went to Aspen. I was dealing with my divorce from Duncan but even more with my brother's decision to leave us all behind. My marriage hadn't survived the anger and pain of losing a brother. As a result of mulling over with Laurie my many questions about life, what I should be doing with my own, and the institution of marriage, both she and her husband began seeing Tom on a regular basis as well. Eventually, I think half my friends started seeing Tom, and I felt I was his agent.

Tom was kind, caring, understanding, and he let me vent, rant, and rage, and it never fazed him. He would look at me with steady eyes, sometimes a slight smile would show if I was really venting my anger, and he'd ask me in the end, "Now . . . how did that feel? I'm still here, aren't I? I haven't left. And that *is* what you are trying to get me to do, isn't it? Well . . . you haven't scared me off yet."

There was always a pause, and my heart would skip a beat, knowing the next line out of his mouth, dreading it.

"It's time for our session to end now, Allison." He would look into my eyes, intentionally trying to let me break the contact first, set my own boundary. My eyes would fill, knowing I wasn't ready to go out into the big, bad world. I wanted to stay safe in this room, to curl up on the couch and go away to a place where I didn't have to pretend I was happy or have any responsibility for myself or others.

I wasn't attracted to Tom sexually, but emotionally I wanted to marry him every day, simply for the gift of caring and accepting me when I couldn't give that to myself. What more could a girl ask for in a man? My joke to my friends back in those days was "Don't get married; just get a therapist. It works." Tom enabled me to begin the process of loving myself in a new way. I began to be honest with myself. He helped me to explore all sides of myself—the compassionate side, the angry, vengeful side, and the lonely child inside a big girl's body that needed tending to. In his office I began to love the little girl and to ask her what she needed. On the day Laurie I and went to the Grand Canyon, she needed to try a new challenge—she was ready to fly.

We pull into the overlooks of the Grand Canyon in the afternoon before going to the campgrounds, get out of our car, and just stare. The massiveness of the canyon hole seems to draw me in. As I get closer and look over the edge I am struck by the stark walls and their vivid coloration—the reds, yellows, and pinks radiating the sun's filtration. I am speechless. It seems so odd to me that despite the colors and beauty of this vast land, I am continually drawn toward the bottom. It doesn't feel positive or negative, only a calling to go deeper than the surface. Tears fill my eyes and again I wonder if the emotions are within me or outside. I sit down, wrap my arms around my knees, and decide to take in what it feels like to feel so small, so insignificant.

Around me, the other tourists are quiet, almost whispering while they take their pictures. There is a hush, a reverence. In a world where we have learned to control so much of our surroundings, here is a place that reminds us there are powers that have been here far longer than we have. It seems to draw thankfulness and humility from me at the same time. I begin to braid my hair, giving myself comfort in the midst of feeling more than I want. I sense many energies emanating from the great canyon and I wonder how to take away the positive ones. I'm at a point of change in my life, and I need its wisdom, not its scars. I send out a silent prayer.

Laurie and I get back in the car to meet Bob and Rebecca at the campsite. After we arrive, we all take a walk together. As we trek through the low brush and parched, cracking earth below, I wonder how something so unattractive on the surface can be so beautiful as a whole. The feelings of anticipation are rising in all of us. Later we organize our packs, try them on to feel the full weight, and go over our lists of food, water, and supplies. Getting our food out to cook our first meal, Laurie and I wonder together about the sanity of our decision to make this trek. We know we are working on a fear of failure we each carry in different forms.

Bob explains to us as we eat dinner at our camp that when he checked us in at the ranger station, they had assigned us an intermediate hike even though he had applied for an easier one. After dinner he shows us the trail map and talks about the terrain. We plan on hiking down in a day, staying on the canyon floor for a day, and then hiking out. As I lean over his shoulder, I see that the name of our hike is Tanner Trail.

I sit there, frozen, not knowing how to react. I have never heard that name until Art told me about his older son, and now it feels all around me. I go to bed thinking about Tanner, trying not to focus on the anxiety I'm having about the hike. I tell myself I'm being silly, making this hike and its name bigger in my mind than necessary. In my heart, hidden away, is a thumping, a knowing.

A trail map I read years later describes Tanner Trail this way: "Unmaintained, very steep near the start, and no water available. Tanner Trail starts at Lipan Point, descends a side canyon, passes around two large mesas then drops more gently through open land to the river. It's an 8 mile route that descends 4,600 feet to the Colorado River. The hike is recommended for the more experienced canyoneer as there is no water and little shade along the path, though the trail is in good condition and relatively easy to follow."

As we will shortly discover, to say that Tanner Trail is steep is an understatement. To say that we are inexperienced hikers is an even greater understatement. We'll just have to take the trail that we've been assigned and make the best of it. I will learn that there is another force at work here. I just don't know it yet.

The next morning my anxiety melts into embarrassment as my three companions give me a hard time about my snoring. I'm told I chased any animal life away with my loud declaration that I was the only one sleeping, as no one else could because of the noise. My mortification is overshadowed by their good humor as they attempt to mimic my sleep sounds. With my face beet red, I laugh as we load our fifty-pound packs into our cars to drive to the South Rim where Tanner Trail begins.

My pack feels awkward as we start the hike, and a part of me just doesn't know if I can really do this. My hikes in Aspen didn't include a heavy pack. I don't know how my shoulders are going to stand up, considering that after one mile they are already sore. I adjust the straps and decide to take my mind off the discomfort and focus on where I am. I'm dropping into this massive canyon and I'm going to feel the water run through my hands at the bottom. I'm going to conquer the fear of not being good enough and in the end say to myself, above all, that I did it. I finished. I am good enough. If only I could believe it right now.

"How do you feel so far, Allison?" Laurie asks.

"I'm okay. This pack isn't fun, but I'm getting used to it. It'll be better after some of the water and food are gone."

"Well, you at least got some sleep!"

Up ahead Bob and Rebecca are signaling a water break. I know the snoring jokes will continue. As we stop, I pretend to lie down and snore.

I take the lead after the break and find myself hiking at a steady pace. We agree in advance when to stop for another water break, so I don't worry about going on ahead. I begin to find a rhythm, a meditation in my own steps. As I look out onto the trail, I start to enjoy myself for the first time. Alone. That in itself is a miracle—that I want to be alone and am enjoying the peace of it. I've been asking for that as a gift from above for the past year. Going to Aspen was part of it. I look up and see a dark-colored bird, very high, flying alone and away from me. I wonder what dark part of me is leaving.

After the second water and snack break we spread out a bit. I find myself alone, with Laurie fairly close behind. The heaviness of the pack is part of my essence now, something I am trying to embrace. I feel like a real hiker, a true explorer, only hours into the trip. I chuckle at that.

Suddenly there's a flash of color in my peripheral vision. I look around. At first I see nothing. Then a figure is in front of me, so real that I even stop for a second in surprise to see another person. Tanner Trail is a lonely one this day, so I am surprised by the appearance of a young boy. Then I realize he's not real but sort of half invisible and almost up in the sky. I shake my head a few times, as if to clear it and make the child go away. The boy stays, but he is gentle in his introduction to me. I remember in elementary school when the movies were on reels. We used to run our fingers through the light from the projector and watch the image move on our hands. The boy is like that—present but not completely in focus. I feel like if I reach out my hand it will go right through him. I can tell he's around nine or ten, but he is not solid in his human form, so it's hard to be sure. He's familiar, and my head and heart begin putting the pieces together. I'm a little afraid, but more than that is my sense of awe.

I look around at my friends, who are hiking close behind me now on the single-track trail, to see if they can see what I am seeing. They are facing him, but it is obvious they aren't seeing him. We stop for a break.

"Laurie, do you see anything unusual?" I ask.

"No. Where?"

"Nothing, I was just checking," I say. I purposefully take long breaths.

We pull out our snacks and water. I eat and drink extra for fear I'm dehydrated. I move closer to Laurie as if to test my own sanity, to hide from the experience. The figure of the boy moves off into the distance. All four of us talk, and I try not to look at him, though my peripheral vision picks up every movement he makes. He never leaves. He seems to be sitting down with his knees together and his chin resting on his hands. He's waiting and watching in such a peaceful way.

When we stop for a late lunch an hour and a half later, I realize I can't ignore this vision any longer. I think to myself, "Why do the really odd things happen to me? How am I going to explain this to anyone, especially Laurie? I already

have her going to my therapist . . . now she'll make Tom
send me off to a loony farm."

"Ah, Laurie?" We are sharing a rock slightly away from
Bob and Rebecca. The heat is intense and we are trying to
find shade.

"Yeah?"

"How's your food?" I chicken out.

"Good." She looks at the nuts in the plastic bag and
looks at me. "Do you want some?"

"No." I take a big breath. "You sure you haven't seen
anything unusual?"

"No. Why? Allison, are you seeing snakes and not
telling me?" She lifts her feet up off the rock.

"No. I was just wondering if you think I'm drinking and
eating enough."

"You're weird, Allison. Yes, you are fine, except when
you think too much." Okay, I decide, that's it for the questions for a while.

Later in the day we spread out more and catch up during breaks. I decide to find out if I truly am crazy, so I begin
to concentrate on the child. His hair is light brown and long.
It is smooth and silky and I have this urge to push it back
from his face. He has soft features and with his longer hair
almost looks like a girl's. He is wearing something yellow,
and though he isn't completely clear to me, I can see and
feel his eyes. I smile at him and say quietly in my mind, but
also out loud, "Hi, Tanner. Why are you here?"

"I need to talk with my dad. I have things I need you to tell him for me and Shea and Mom." From that point on he answers me through his eyes and his mind. His lips don't move. I just know inside what he is saying, though it isn't audible. The words are as clear as if he is talking, but words aren't needed, only his heart, his emotions. When I can't understand him, a picture is given to me. His eagerness to communicate is contagious.

I'm not scared because I know right away that he is here out of love, out of longing. Tears fill my eyes. I'd have given anything for a message from Rod, and I want to grant this opportunity for Art. It is as if some hidden part of me knew this would happen, and I am strangely relieved that it has begun. The only thing I fear is that I have lost my mind or have been imagining the whole thing for selfish reasons. I tell Tanner this. I also decide it's time for a witness.

"Laurie, I know you'll think I'm crazy, but I'm seeing Tanner, Art's deceased son." I look into her eyes to make sure she is with me in the conversation. Her eyes get bigger but I can feel her open heart.

"Well . . . what is he like? What is he saying?" she asks. She trusts the look in my eye. "Are you sure?"

"Yes, I am." I pause and let it sink in for my sake as much as hers. "He's here because he wants Art to know where they all are and what it's like. He's missing him and needs to let him know he's always with him. He looks a lot like the picture Art showed me."

"Can you see him clearly? Where is he now?" Laurie's voice is soft, compassionate. Her own faith gives her the openness to believe.

"He's right over there, near that cloud. He is sort of half visible." I point and she tries to see. Her belief is a gift.

Silence.

"Allison, is he with God?" her voice breaks.

"I see the place. It must be with God. It's a definite heaven. He's actually in a separate space now, but he is right next to where Shea is in this place." I have to slow myself down. I feel I am bursting with emotions. "He's so sad to be away from his dad, Laurie. He's desperate to communicate."

Laurie and I hike quietly for a while. In a few minutes I say, "Laurie, up ahead in a half mile there will be a stack of rocks and yellow flowers next to them. The flowers are a gift to me from him." I'm sure Laurie is questioning, and I'm scared they won't be there. I need them to be there to know this is real.

When we see the rocks and the small yellow flowers growing next to them, we stop and look at one another and smile. As we hike on, the tears come and I can't stop them. I never talk to Bob and Rebecca about what is happening; it is too private. I can barely admit it to myself. As I hike on, I know they wonder what is going on with me.

"Tanner, tell me where you are now. What is it like there?" I ask.

He can't find words, so he shows me. The picture is not only visual but an actual emotion. I see a place where the children are. They are all doing things, very busy, and un-aware that I'm looking on from far away. There is no audible music, but I can feel it. They seem to be doing things they love to do or have always wanted to do. One girl is sliding down a slide with her hands raised and a huge smile on her face. Tanner tells me she was crippled while on earth and now she is free to run and play. There are no limitations, no barriers. It's like being taken to a pretend land of dreams. I can feel great joy, wholeness. I look at Tanner, asking him if these children have all died. The answer is yes. I wonder if they are still sad about being taken away from their families. His answer is in two parts. Yes, they miss the people they are away from, but they know in a different way than we can un-derstand that there will be an eternity together. This is what enables them to be joyful and to carry out their dreams, to do the things they missed out on while alive. Their sadness is for those still missing them, for their pain. They know this is only the beginning of the longing, not the end.

It is clear that Tanner is not fully in this place yet; he is in between. He hasn't yet taken the jump. His emotions aren't resolved. Looking into his eyes the anger is clear. He needs to show it to me, but not yet. He looks away so I won't see too much. He instantly changes the mood and I follow him in it.

Tanner then begins telling me things about his dad. I can see things they did together as a family—camping, snowboarding, and games in the yard. He shows me the depth of his dad's heart, the authenticity. The pictures are like an old silent movie where no words are needed to understand the depth of feeling, the intent. More attention is needed to watch every detail, to notice the actions, the touch that only love brings. Kisses, holding, playing all unfold into memories that transcend death.

I can tell he is trying to get me to like his father. In my mind I communicate to him that I am attracted to his dad but feel uncomfortable since he has just lost his wife and kids. He understands but lets me know it is okay. I see in his mischievous smile that he has plans. He begins to tell me things about himself, that yellow is his favorite color and the yellow fleece he is wearing now was his favorite before he died. He tells me Shea had one like it that was red. He shows me Shea's independence, his charm.

The mood changes again. Tanner has messages for his dad. There is so much more he wants to experience and share with him. There is more joy he wants to give him as a son. He wants to feel his dad's pride again, to be on the mountain with him snowboarding through the trees, smiling and feeling free together. There is a longing to feel his hands on his face and to listen to him sing before he says goodnight. His sorrow and frustration are heavy weights between us in this space.

Tanner tells me that there will be a big rock up ahead. I will know it when I see the clearing.

"Laurie, tell Bob and Rebecca we are going to take a break up ahead. There's a clearing and we can stop there," I say. All three are behind me. My feet don't move fast enough to keep up with Tanner. Every time I stop, I realize that my toes and feet are in pain. While I communicate with Tanner I am oblivious to the pain.

"Sure. How do you know there's a clearing?" she asks.

"Tanner is telling me." I once again hope it will be true, but my doubt is small.

After talking with Laurie a few minutes, I can't slow my pace. It helps to stay in the zone I have been taken to in order to fully hear Tanner. I can't even begin to share it fully with Laurie, so I don't even try. I walk on ahead, wondering what I will see. I begin to see an opening to the canyon walls. It's the clearing. My heart speeds up. I come closer, praying for a sign, slowing down. I reach the bend, and there beyond the opening is a big rock form protruding out of the canyon wall. I stare and allow the tears to fill my eyes. It means something enormous. It looks like a boulder falling from the wall, while in reality it's a part of the formation. I take my pack off, the weight feeling light compared to the weight of the rock in front of me. My whole body is drawn toward the mass. I sit alone staring, not able to look away, glad I am alone. Within minutes I see Tanner hitting and screaming at the boulder, crying out in fierce anger. "I hate this rock! I hate leaving. I hate you, rock, I hate you. You took us away. You ruined my life. I want my dad back!" I weep for him, for all of the unfair loss in the world.

There is nothing I can do but be there with him. This is anger well deserved. My heart is broken for all four of them. I know all I can do is just be there and try to remember every detail to tell Art how much Tanner hurts in being taken away. Tanner needs his dad to know these things so much that he has brought me to the Grand Canyon. I feel like it is the reason I am here.

When Laurie finds me and sees the rock, she is taken aback as well. She sees my tears.

"Tell me about it," she says, touching my hand. We move closer to the edge.

"Tanner is furious at the rock for killing him. Can you see the formation of the rock?" I ask.

"Yes."

"Well," I say, "he just showed me how deeply he hates being gone from Art."

"That is amazing that he is showing you all of this, Allison," she says. "What a gift."

"I don't fully understand it." I pause. "But I want to."

Bob and Rebecca come up and we all rest, though I am coming out of my skin from the experience. I walk around to push away the tears, the intensity. Tanner is gone for a while and as I look at the formation all I can see is the authenticity of his ache. My fragile heart is thankful for Laurie's willingness to believe and to keep the experience between the two of us.

"Is this a religious experience?" she asks as we walk away from the formation. I have to laugh. "I don't know! It's something but I'm not sure what!"

"Well, I'm not ready for this in my life yet," she says.

I'm sure she wonders if it is something she can "catch"

from me—like the whole therapy bug. Poor thing, she has no idea what to do with her outrageous friend who at least keeps life interesting.

Tanner continues to tell me what is ahead every once in a while. His mood has shifted back to love, and on some level I know that the anger is just something he needed to feel and release. He tells me about small purple flowers I will see, and when the switchbacks are coming up on the trail. In the beginning it is for proof; later it is a game. His sense of humor is playful, engaging, and even sneaky at times. It takes my mind off my aching feet. I know my toe-nails will fall off within weeks. There are few flowers on the trail these hot May days, but the ones I see are bursts of color in an achingly barren, lonely area. At one point I see Tanner holding a small bouquet out for me, a big smile on his face. If not before, I am now smitten.

I ask Tanner about Shea. He isn't as reachable to me. Tanner points his hand to a space in the open sky. Like the opening of a computer screen from dark to color with the push of the mouse, I can see a group of children similar to the ones I had seen earlier. It wasn't there before and I am not able to comprehend how all of a sudden I am able to see it, but as I watch it doesn't matter. My soul is drawn to Shea immediately; there is no question which one he is.

Shea is off to the side and is dancing with other chil-dren. They are all holding hands, although sometimes Shea is dancing alone. I watch him, wondering if I have ever seen a more beautiful child. His long, deep brown hair is like silk, and when he throws his head back, it looks like a halo. I want to touch him, experience him. A smile spreads through my whole body as I watch his joy and freedom. Love, as well as a quiet independence, radiates from him. I look back at Tanner, appreciating their differences. Tanner is wise, soulful. He carries a weight on his shoulders. Shea is exuberant, filled with self-assured belonging. Tanner communicates that Shea will be okay but that his "missing" is different. It's about a bond that was an extraordinary gift from birth. Tanner can't find words for it, and I am unable to understand it fully because I have never known this kind of love.

Shea looks so happy where he is that I wonder how he can be so happy and so sad at the same time. He doesn't look sad, but the longer I look at him there is something in me that can sense it. It is a knowing that I can't explain. Tanner shows me that the missing, the yearning, the love, is carried in Shea's soul. It is his essence and it will never change. This place (heaven, I guess, for lack of any other term) is about healing and joy and wholeness. And it's so much more. Shea now knows that he will be with his dad soon enough and that this is the place for him to live his dreams. Time is not a factor because it is not a reality here. All he knows is that they will be together again, and then for a long, long time. The longing to be with his dad won't leave, but his God will heal him with love.

Kathy is way off to one side and seems on her own journey. It's as if she is aware of her children but is also letting them go so they can travel their own paths. She has healing of her own to tend to. It isn't time for me to know her yet. She purposely lets the boys do the communicating with me. And though I have the strongest communication with Tanner, I always feel Shea. Shea's missing of his dad is raw and fresh and formless while Tanner's has transformed to a mission, a determination.

As we reach the bottom of the hike down, all I want is the pack off my back and my hiking boots far, far away. Laurie and I soak our feet in the cool water of the Colorado River. Bob and Rebecca join us and we talk about where to camp and what to eat. We're all so excited to have made it. We don't want to think about the trip back out, but because it has taken us so long to get down we decide to leave the next day and take two days to climb back to the rim. In the late afternoon light the canyon walls radiate color. I look out onto the waters wondering what it would feel like to see the canyon from a raft. I am ready for one to float by and ask me if I want a ride out.

"Allison, you need to write all this down," Laurie says as we wade through the shallows.

"I know. A pen and paper weren't exactly on my list of things to bring. Do you have anything?"

"No," she says.

I look in the front pouch of my pack where I had put the keys to our rental car, and there is a small notepad and a pencil. "Laurie, you're not going to believe it! I don't remember packing this." I will never know how they got there.

After setting up camp and preparing our freeze-dried dinner, I go off by myself to write. I'm sticky with sweat, and dust covers my face despite being washed off once; being dirty has never felt so rewarding. I take a flashlight and write down as many details as I can for Art. A light breeze seems to come out of nowhere to cool my sunburned shoulders. I stop writing every few minutes to try to remember every detail and to listen to the night sounds. The water trickles by softly and the canyon seems alive. The high walls echo every sound, proclaiming their power. I think of my experience that day and wonder what these walls would tell me if they could talk. As I resume writing, I feel a little crazy. Later, as I drift off to sleep, praying I won't snore, I wonder if Tanner will be with me the next day or if our visit is over.

I wake up to a very sore body. I pop some Advil and rub my feet and legs. I try to decide which is more important, the rubbing or a cup of coffee. The coffee wins. As I sit up and begin to move I dread the thought of hiking again. I can't feel any presence and the world doesn't seem any different. I wonder if the whole experience was no more than a dream.

I drink my coffee and look around at the exquisite morning light on the canyon walls. I pick up the hot cup and go to sit by the water. I wonder how many others have been to this exact spot, how many other lives I share it with. The canyon, in all of its beauty, its vastness, its emptiness, its ancient stories, is a deep and abiding gift to all who come. The land itself seems to ask something from you, to demand that you give of yourself emotionally as well as physically. After packing up and finally getting back on the trail, I begin to come alive again.

As we ascend the canyon, I try to focus on climbing as best I can considering that I have broken a toenail at the quick and my foot is throbbing. I'm reeling from the previous day's experiences and trying my best to put them in a place where I can examine them later. Laurie, Bob, Rebecca, and I share our meals and our struggles to get back up out of the canyon, talking only of practicalities. God bless Bob, our personal camel, who carries pounds and pounds of filtered water on his back so we can all survive. By the time we find a place to camp for the night, there are few words left to utter among us.

On the third day I find myself flying up the steepest switchbacks, the toughest climbs. At one extremely challenging point, Laurie and Rebecca are scared and crying, and I know I should be too. The trail is thin and the drop-off is far. There is little margin for error and falling would be fatal, I'm sure. Our legs are shaking, making it harder to stay stable, focused. Yet I feel Tanner. I talk to him in my mind, words coming back to me I know are his. He talks me through the fear.

"You can do this. You are brave—braver than you've known. Just believe in yourself." He has me encourage the others and pass on his strength. As we hike on, I can't stop my feet from moving. I have so much energy. During the rest of the hike out, he is simply my friend.

When I reach the top I am way ahead of the others. I set my pack down, loosen my boots, sit down and cry. An overwhelming sense of love comes over me. I have experienced something beyond my imagination. I met Art's little boys and received messages for him. As I wait for the others, I wonder how I am going to tell Art what I've seen.

Laurie gets to the top, crying with exhaustion. Bob and Rebecca are close behind. Our trek completed, we all share in the sense of accomplishment but even more in the relief that it is over. As we hug our good-byes, I still reveal nothing to Bob or Rebecca.

Laurie and I decide to take pictures of each other beside the sign: TANNER TRAIL. We walk to our rental car in the nearby parking lot and can't find the keys. Bob and Rebecca have already driven off, and we're in a panic. I set my pack next to the car, rummage through the pack's front pocket, where I had put them when we started out, and all of a sudden I understand.

"Laurie, I'll be right back," I say.

"Where are you going, Allison? We have to find our keys."

"I have an idea. Wait here."

I go down to the Tanner Trail sign and look in the place I think I remember putting my pack down while waiting for the others. I don't see anything. My worry increases. I listen. I look in the bushes off to the side of the sign. There they are.

"Tanner, thank you. Thank you for everything. I promise

I will tell your dad everything. I loved meeting you. You will always stay in my heart. Tell Shea I feel the same." I say these things aloud to Tanner quietly.

I close my eyes, taking in the moment. The late afternoon sun is beating down on my back as I look again at the sign. Tanner Trail. Something is being asked of me, something important. It goes beyond simply accepting this experience. As I pause before returning to the car I think it must be a little like the magic in *Peter Pan*. In order to fly, the children must clap their hands and say, "I believe."

As I look at the keys in my hand and look back to where I found them, I realize they were nowhere close to where I had laid my pack down. I smile to myself, feel the peace and run back to Laurie and the car.

"Where were the keys?" she asks. "How did you find them?"

"Off in the bushes, Laurie. Tanner showed me where they were."

"Oh." She stares. "Wow."

"Yeah, he just wanted me to come back so he could say good-bye."

Laurie looks at me and says, "I'll stop at the nearest pay phone so you can call Art." We get in the car and begin to drive. "What is that conversation going to be like?"

I have the little notebook in my hand and am wondering the same thing. "I think it will be good, Laurie. I think he'll believe in it."

"Holland and Hart, may I help you?" It is the same voice that had answered my first call to Art's office after he wrote back to me.

"Yes, this is Allison Snyder. Is Art Daily available?"

"Yes, one moment, please," she says.

"Allison, where are you? Are you out of the canyon?" I can tell Art is happy to hear from me.

"Yes. Art, I have the most amazing story to tell you. I'm still in the park grounds at a pay phone. Laurie's in the car. Please stay open to this. I don't know how to start. I just spent the last few days with Tanner and Shea. They came to me, and I need to tell you all of their messages for you." Tears begin to flow. The magnitude of all that has happened overwhelms me.

"Okay. I'm here." His voice is kind, if a little hesitant.

I tell Art the story from beginning to end. Through the phone I can feel his emotion. "Art, Tanner pointed out the fleeces they were wearing. He said they were their favorites. Tanner's was yellow, and Shea's was red."

"Oh my God, Allison, I just packed those away the other day, along with some of their other special things. I'm amazed you've actually seen them."

"You know, Art, I had the sense that Tanner was trying to provide some details to prove to you—and to me—that my experience with him was real. He also showed me a long lake bordered by high canyon walls and a white speedboat floating in a quiet cove. You were in the boat, with Shea and Tanner. It felt like a happy, quiet time for the three of you."

"Yeah," says Art, a note of awe in his voice, "that's Lake Powell. I have a boat there, and we would drive down occasionally in the summer and fall. In the evenings when I took the boys fishing, Kathy would stay on the houseboat that we would anchor in some remote canyon. It was a special place for all of us. We'd water ski and wave board in the early mornings when the water was so smooth it was like skiing on velvet."

The particulars about the boys and their experiences with him, as well as his own gut instinct and desire to believe, are beginning to persuade Art that this really happened. He especially understands Tanner's anger at the rock in the canyon, though it is painful to relate and difficult for Art to hear. I have no idea how long we talk, only that I bring his boys back to him in some small way. It is a beginning.

That night in a hotel room with Laurie before drifting off to sleep I clap my hands and quietly claim to the darkness, "I believe. I believe." I sense that a large part of Art does, too.

Somewhere above, Tanner and Shea smile.

State of Wonder

In my lifetime I won't receive another call like this
one. I'm sitting in my office immersed in the business affairs
of my clients, and I suddenly find myself listening to Allison's
extraordinary story of her encounters with Tanner and Shea
along the Tanner Trail in the Grand Canyon. I've never had any
visions of my own, or visits from people who have passed on, so
my belief system has nothing to hang on to, no frame of reference. What is this all about? How could Allison have learned
so much about us, so many personal things, unless Tanner really appeared to her? I suppose it could be many things, but a
quiet voice within me, a voice that I have not listened to before,
seems to be saying, "Art, existence is far wider and deeper
than what you have known, and death is not what it appears. It
may be, in truth, a state of perfect grace, and beauty, and
hope, and of infinite possibilities. Tanner and Shea are trying
to open you to these things. Put aside what you believe and
open your heart. They need you."

I understand Tanner's sadness and anger, and every

ounce of me wants to take him in my arms and protect him from this grief—to have him with me again. Allison believes that his anger was more a symbol of his love for me, his longing. When I asked Allison about her sense that he is between places, she assured me that he is only staying to watch over me. She feels he has been allowed to stay present for a short while to make sure that I am okay and that he will move on soon.

While I can't say that it comes easily to me, or without elements of doubt, in accepting Allison's experience I find myself in a state of wonder and faith that is surprisingly refreshing. My soul feels like a pond full of tiny silverfish, leaping and glittering in the sun. What a wild place to be, so locked down in emptiness and grief, and yet so close to and so embraced by the ones for whom I grieve.

Far Island

SEVERAL MONTHS HAVE PASSED, AND I'VE RETURNED TO
work full time. I'm hanging out in the evenings with Piper or
Pandora, and I've read almost everything that has been written on the death of a child. Each speaks of an unbearable
loss, a death that is beyond understanding or meaning and
that is out of the course of normal human events. A child is
not supposed to die before his parents. Not ever.

I continue my sessions twice a week with Brad Ham. I
am slowly rising out of the darkness, and I feel as if I have
come to a place of waiting, a time between things. Brad tells
me that classical psychology calls this "liminal space," in
which the psyche regroups and readies itself for whatever may
happen next. It is a time in which great healing can occur,
and in which the soul may even be reborn. I know only that I
am stronger and that Kathy and Tanner and Shea and I are
becoming more accepting of the awful changes that have
taken place and with our new way of being. I tell Brad that I
sometimes seem to experience sorrow and joy all at the same

time, and I ask him how that is possible. Brad responds, "There may be hope for you yet, Art. Intense feelings are not mutually exclusive, and despite what most of us believe, we do not have to complete our experience with a current emotion in order to be able to feel its opposite. The potential for the full range of human feelings is present at all times within us, and the more available we are to them, the healthier we are emotionally. So stay open to it as best you can."

I also tell Brad a lot about Allison, and I explore with him the conflict that I'm having with how quickly she has come into my life. Brad respects Allison's deep intuitiveness and her experiences with Tanner and Shea and Kathy, and once again he encourages me to be as open as I possibly can to these seemingly unusual happenings. Brad tells me there are certain people in this world who see and hear things, and perhaps even know things, that the rest of us don't; in his view it is a great blessing that Allison has come into my life. His simple advice in the matter is "Follow your heart, wherever it leads you. There are no other rules."

Allison is back home in Austin taking some time off before moving on to Dallas, and we need to figure out what comes next. We're sure we want to spend more time together, and she can always visit me again in Aspen. But Aspen is a tough environment for us. I've lived here for a long time, and I have a lot of friends and acquaintances and a lot of personal history. And because of the accident, no matter where we go or what we do, the focus will be too much on me. The house is full of ghosts and memories, and the community continues to be attentive to my well-being. It's not judgment; it's just awareness and caring. There is nowhere for us to be really alone, and it must be incredibly difficult for Allison. She's living in the shadows and reflections of my lost family, and there is little opportunity for her to raise her arms to the sky and dance her own dance.

Back in the late 1970s and early '80s I used to hang out in St. Barth's, in the Lesser Antilles, when I had vacation time. I spent an entire three-month sabbatical there in 1982, bringing Piper with me over the Christmas holidays and then flying back with her to St. Thomas, where United Airlines took over, and returning to the island on my own. St. Maarten and Anguilla are the other islands in the group. I've never been to Anguilla, although it is reputed to have only a few scattered resorts and to be ringed by long, lonely beaches of incredibly fine white sand. This was to have been another sabbatical year for me (the firm allows one every five years for partners), and we had made family plans to go to Disney World and then to fly down to Anguilla to check it out. Those plans have been long canceled, but I begin thinking again about Anguilla and I finally get up the courage to call Allison and ask her if she would be willing to spend a couple of weeks on a far island with me. Surprisingly, she says she'll think about it, and a couple of days later she calls to say that she's decided to throw caution to the winds and to roll the long dice. In her words, "Spending fourteen days on a deserted island with a man I barely know is bound to tell me something."

Suddenly I'm so excited I can't sit still. I've heard about

a small, twelve-unit resort called Shoal Bay Villas, which has one-bedroom and studio apartments with kitchens and is located right on the beach at Shoal Bay East. The beach is said to be one of the five most beautiful in the world, so I decide I can't go too far wrong and I book us for two weeks, starting in about ten days. It's the off-season in the Caribbean, and reservations are easy to come by. I set it up so that we will meet in Miami, spend the night in the airport hotel, and then continue on down to the islands in the morning.

Real Flying

I'm sitting in the Miami airport waiting for Art's plane from Denver to come in. We're meeting here before going on to San Juan and then Anguilla. What am I doing? I'm meeting a man I hardly know and going to some island God knows where, *and* I am spending two whole weeks with him?

What if we don't get along? What if he repulses me? What if I repulse him? What if I snore?

Even though we've had the weekend together in Aspen and a number of long phone conversations since my trip out of the Grand Canyon, I'm nervous about being alone with Art for such an extended period of time. I'm not the only one who's nervous. My family and close friends are a bit worried about how quickly the relationship is moving along. They know my sojourn in Aspen has been good for me, but my coming home and going right back to visit Art, whom I met the night before I returned to Austin, does have them wondering. When I announce I'm going to an island they've never heard of with him, my friends Kathy and Laurie take me out to dinner for a "drill session." After spending two hours in the restaurant, we sit in Laurie's car in my driveway and talk for another hour. Laurie was there in the canyon and has some history on Art and his family. Kathy, whom I also know from teaching tennis at the club, wants to make sure this isn't a rebound for Art. Throughout the evening I see them exchange glances. I know they are skeptical but trying not to quash my enthusiasm. But I also know that's because they want only the best for me, and that feels good.

A day or two later, as I'm packing for the trip to Anguilla, my parents come up to my room and sit on my bed.

My mom takes a deep breath and then says quietly, "Allison, are you sure about this? This is so unlike you."

"I know," I say. I can see the concern in their eyes. They have watched the video of Kathy, Shea, and Tanner's memorial service and talked briefly with Art on the phone. That is all they know of him. I know they think I've allowed myself to move too quickly.

"We just want to make sure you have thought this through, that you realize all this man has gone through. Are you ready for this?" my mom asks.

My dad is there to support her and me as well. "Allison, we just want the best. This seems like a lot to get involved with."

I stop rummaging in the closet for my black skirt and sit on the floor near my parents. I love them. I love the way they care about me and yet want to give me space. I realize that Rod's death has left them with scars that will never heal; they must be worrying that another child will go off the deep end. Though we have talked quite a bit about Art, his situation and my growing feelings for him, I haven't been very detailed (they're my parents, after all) nor shared with them my experience at the Grand Canyon. But I know this is an important time to express what I feel. We are all nervous and want to say the right thing.

"Okay. I can't say for sure that I know what I am doing. I can't say that I'm not excited to go off to some exotic island." I pull my thoughts together. "I just have this gut feeling, this strong sense that I have to do this. I just know it. I would never have chosen to get involved with a man who had all this happening in his life. I don't completely understand what I'm feeling, but I know I have to go and find out. I promise to call you and keep you updated."

We hug after talking some more, and, though I know their doubts still remain, I think they know I'll be true to myself.

Now that I'm at the airport, I vacillate between listening to my instincts—which are telling me this is a cool thing—and freaking out because our relationship has progressed so quickly. Since deciding to take this trip I've written half a dozen lengthy letters telling him all of my deep secrets (I snore) and fears (not being in control), mainly so that he won't be too surprised by the real me.

I've been thinking a lot since my return from the Grand Canyon about the fact that I've had strong intuitive experiences throughout my life. Déjà vu moments occur at least once a week; other times I have premonitional dreams or I find myself in situations where I know what is going to happen next. I can finish sentences for people or know what they should do with a problem based on my inner voice. I haven't focused on it much up until now, and my need to control everything has probably held me back from pursuing it. Since my trip to the Canyon (where I definitely felt I lost control in a new way), it feels stronger, elevated, especially in relation to Art. There is almost an urgency within me to "listen," and I clearly want to know this man even deeper.

There is a lot of intimacy with Art in our talks. While we are becoming very close friends, we are both aware of the physical attraction as well. There don't seem to be many barriers between us. Though part of me is still scared and nervous about being involved with him, like a child jumping into the water for the first time, an even greater part of me feels confident about what lies ahead. I feel as if I'm being led by something greater than myself. I'm ready to jump.

Now my hands are sweating and I have to go to the ladies' room. I am determined to be at the baggage claim, where we agreed to meet, when he comes down the escalator. If I go to the bathroom now, I may miss him. I know his flight has arrived, so he should be here soon. "What are you doing here, Allison?" By this time I'm talking out loud to myself. It feels as if I've gone temporarily insane.

"Allison." It's his voice. I turn around and there he is. He looks even better than before, his eyes bright. His medium build is solid, lean. He's dressed in his usual jeans,

Abercrombie shirt, and tennis shoes. His gray hair is scrambled. I love that he is a successful attorney and yet he looks like Dennis the Menace, casually rumpled. He dresses only to please himself and wears what feels comfortable. There are no pretenses, and as I watch him, I hope someday I'll come to the same place in my own life.

"Art . . . hi."

All of the fear is gone as I smile and hug him. I look into his eyes and I know exactly why I am here, why I have decided to give this relationship a chance.

"How are you, girl?" He stops to kiss me with just enough meaning to show me he is happy to see me.

"I'm great, now. But I've been nervous, so nervous, that now I have to pee. I'll be right back." I head to the bathroom in a sprint and I hear his soft laughter behind me.

I come out and look at him as I walk toward him. Though he is in his midfifties he looks forty. He's searching for his luggage on the carousel. I approach slowly. I am utterly amazed at his beauty. His face shines with a sense of openness and caring I have never seen in another. How is he so kind, so good? How can he smile so through the misery I know he carries inside? I want to know this man.

The next day as we sit next to each other on the flight to San Juan, I look at him reading his book and wonder to myself, "Is he nervous? What is he thinking about this crazy trip we are taking?" So I ask him.

Art touches my arm and leans in close to my face so that our noses are almost touching. We are sitting in the two seats between the aisle and the window, but we may as well be in a cozy room by ourselves. The sunlight is coming in through the window. He pulls his reading glasses off, marks the page with his bookmark, sets the book aside, and smiles into my eyes. His words are deliberate. "Allison, nothing could make me happier than being on this plane with you. Am I nervous?" He pauses and thinks, while his glasses dangle from his fingers. "Maybe a little. But I have nothing to lose. I've lost everything already. I have no one close except my daughter, Piper. In some strange way I feel I'm starting over. I have no attachments to anything. When you wrote me that first letter, I decided to take a chance again. Now you are, too. I think we both know we were meant to meet. I guess what I want is to see where it all leads."

There are tears in my eyes as I gaze at him and wonder if he's for real. I have looked my whole life for a man to be this open and honest with how he feels and what he wants.

"Oh." I'm speechless, a rare occurrence for me.

"Are you okay with all of this, Allison?" he asks.

"Yes. No. I don't know how to describe what I'm feeling. Overwhelmed is a good word." I pause. I have been waiting to say this in person. "I look at you and all of your pain frightens me. Your strength in the midst of that pain overpowers me. I feel mushy inside when I look at you now. I still wonder if it's okay to feel these things for a man who has just lost his wife and two children. On top of that, I have just had a powerful experience with your sons and I'm beginning to wonder whether I've lost my mind completely." I smile.

He strokes my arm and then leans over to kiss me. In that moment I know I've completely fallen for him.

"The experience happened for a reason. We both know it was real. We'll talk more about all of it. We have a lot of time to get to know each other." He reaches out to hold my hand. "Now, what I want you to do is just take a deep breath, relax, and let this unravel as it will. If my family is really a part of this, they will show us the way. Believe me, with Kathy's spirit around, there is no doubt she'll let us know how she feels."

We smile at each other and I turn to jelly inside and finally turn back to reading my magazine. As I pretend to concentrate, my heart beats rapidly against my chest and I can feel my reddened face burning. All I can think is "I've found him. If he is for real, I've found him."

Anguilla

We get out of the cab, put our bags down near the office check-in, and walk toward the beach. As our plane dropped into the Anguilla airport half an hour before, we could see the magnificent beaches. All we want now is to touch one and see that it is real. Coming through the courtyard of the villas, I feel my jaw drop. The water is four shades of blue, all of them vibrant, intense. The sand is pure white, and the water goes on forever. It makes the earth seem flat. Warmth spreads around and through me and I realize it is the soft breeze that has already drawn me in. I feel as if we have come to a different world, to a place where God painted all of my favorite colors to his perfection. Very few people are on the beach as we take our shoes off and step into the calm waters. Water tickles my feet at first touch and I reach down to sift the sand through my fingers. The quietness of the island feels sacred.

The Shoal Bay Villas are quaint, unassuming, and ideal for two people getting to know one another. Like Art and his taste, they are unpretentious but elegant. The rooms are small and clean. The stark white walls accent the white wicker couches and chairs covered in bright island prints. Haitian art decorates the walls, mirroring the views outside.

The kitchen is well equipped, so we decide to eat breakfasts and lunches in the room and have our dinners out. We make a list for the grocery store, sharing each of our favorite foods. Later we walk the beach, and when we lie on the recliners we plug a Y-jack into the radio and listen to music together.

Our villa has a porch overlooking the beach. There is a smooth white table with two white chairs. We eat breakfast and lunch there every day and play card games after going out at night. Art teaches me cribbage and I want to play all the time. The conversations in the evening are intimate, even heavy, like the night around us.

The morning after we arrive, Art is leaning against the balcony, staring out over the sea. "What are you thinking?" I ask.

"About them," he says quietly.

"What about?" I am sitting in a chair, my legs propped up next to where he is standing.

"How much they would have loved it here." His voice breaks. "How much fun it would be to chase them down the beach or to snorkel together."

There is a family playing in the water down the beach. "I wish I could be them." It is the truth.

The sun breaks through the morning haze, the clouds parting. I pick up my sunglasses on the table next to me and put them on to cover the lone tear that has fallen. We sit in the lonely silence, wishing it away.

That night I go onto the balcony after we come home from dinner. The sun is setting gently. The ocean is soon shrouded in darkness, and my imagination takes over. I shut my eyes and think of the entire colonies alive in the ocean. I wonder how many waves come to shore each night. With my eyes closed, the sound of the surf is exaggerated. The word *healing* comes to my mind. The thick air and the surf breed a quietness in me. I find stillness in the solitude that punctures the hurt in my soul and allows me to bleed slowly. The pain that has been hiding deep inside for so long begins to seep out, a bit at a time. I realize that for the first time I feel safe enough to let it go. The safety is from within as well as from our talks and the courage I see radiating out of Art. Though I know he has joined me on the porch, we are not touching. In the midst of my emotions I look over and see tears running down his face. I stare at him and say a silent prayer. Release and heal. Release and heal. The waves seem to be calling out to me as they hit the shoreline. The soft wind blows lightly as if its only purpose is to dry the tears. I share the silence with him, trying not to rescue him with my touch. This ache comforts him; it allows him to feel his loved ones. I am connected to him in a way I've never experienced with anyone before.

There is a garden reef two hundred yards away from shore directly out from our beach. It sits there quietly, almost asking for people to see its treasure. Though I see the water breaking against the reef, I have no idea what I will find the first time we snorkel out there. As I kick my fins, listening to the splash against the water, I feel a little nervous. I've never snorkeled before and the equipment is awkward at first. Art teaches me how to clean my mask with spit and how to breathe through the snorkel. The warm water pushes against my skin as we head out toward the reef. Art takes my hand as we get closer and we watch a new world unfold. Rainbows of fish, all shapes and sizes, envelop us. The schools of fish stay together, seeming to communicate telepathically so that they all move in the same direction exactly at the same time. The fish pick at the coral with their lips, grabbing the food needed for the day. From the corner of their eyes they watch us, making sure we aren't dangerous. Every once in a while a fish almost runs into me, its bulging eyes popping out farther, surprised to find something so strange looking at it. Yellows swim by, then blues, then black striped fish. I can't stop laughing from sheer joy. I feel as if I'm in the middle of a painting. As Art and I swim around the reef and point at each unusual fish, I feel like a mermaid who has found her home. I never want to leave this place of color and silence. When we come up to the surface and talk, careful not to touch the coral, we agree to visit each day. We put our faces back in the water and hold hands, swimming into the colors. My favorite becomes a gray, thin, long-nosed creature called a trumpet fish, which looks so silly and out of place that I love it instantly.

After snorkeling we lie in the sun. I ask Art to put

sunscreen on my back and then marvel at the way he massages me. It is the giddiness of a crush, the enjoying of every move that he makes. My body responds to his presence, his touch.

We hang out on the white sand, reading books until we bake and then chase one another into the water. The cool blue water washes away the heat. I wrap my legs around his waist and float on my back with my arms stretched out wide. My hair, whitening in the sun, floats and grazes against my shoulders. I pull myself up and intertwine my fingers around Art's neck and stare at him before we kiss.

"I'm really starting to like you, ya know?" I say.

"Don't worry, it's mutual."

"Thanks for all of this." I pause, trying to find better words. "It's amazing . . . all of it."

"Thanks for coming with me." He smiles back.

I lean back again in the water, my legs still wrapped around his waist. I feel blessed. I remind myself not to fight it, to breathe.

We have such big hurdles in front of us, and yet while we walk the beach and talk every day, sharing honestly and clearly who we have become—the ways in which he failed Kathy, how I failed Duncan—we can both feel the shift happening. The friendship is deepening. We ask hard questions of one another and hurt one another with the answers at times. We are committed to honesty.

"What do you regret most about your relationship with Kathy?" I ask one day as we walk the shoreline. I wrap my fingers in his and pull him closer to the water. I love the sinking feeling beneath my toes as the water recedes back from shore.

"You don't mess around, do you?" Art says with a smile. He looks out at the water, gives my hand a squeeze and says, "I guess I regret that we had built patterns in our marriage and they prevented us, me, from being really intimate. I know she had issues with her dad, but I never encouraged her to talk about it. I acted in ways that pushed her buttons and she did the same to me. There were times we were close. Before she died we seemed very close. I just wish I had appreciated her more for who she was. I wish I could've seen more of her pain." He pauses to look out at the ocean and then at me. "She could be difficult but she was such a good woman. I can see that more clearly now that she is gone. I guess what I can see is what I contributed to the unhealthiness."

"You miss her a lot, don't you?" I ask. I don't want to hear the answer because I already know it.

"Yes, very much, but not like the kids. I miss her friendship, her humor." He looks at me to gauge my reaction.

We walk in silence and my stomach tightens. I notice that I have tensed up so much that my neck hurts. I move my head side to side, willing the anxiety away. I've got to come to terms with my jealousy of Kathy, I realize. I struggle with thinking I have no right to feel this way and yet I do. I'm aware that if Art and I continue to get closer she'll be in my life as well. I decide to accept this confusion. I take a deep breath and force my shoulders to release. I choose to embrace her and the memory of her, instead of fighting her.

I stop to pick up a shell that's caught between my toes. I look at Art and can see he is letting me process my thoughts. I'm sure he is wondering if it is safe to continue on.

"How about you? What do you regret about your marriage?" he asks.

"This is hard," I say, smiling a big smile, and we both laugh.

"It is . . . but it's good. Now go ahead."

"That's a complicated question because I'm still trying to figure it out. I guess I'd have to say that I regret how I ended it, how I handled that part." I feel flustered trying to explain so much when it is all scrambled in my brain. I take a deep breath. "I blamed Duncan for everything, I made myself the victim, and I blamed the failure of our marriage on Rod's suicide."

"So what was the real failure?" he asks.

"Me. I failed." Be honest, I remind myself. Even if it means rejection. "I didn't know who I was anymore after Rod's death. It was like getting slapped in the face. I didn't know anything anymore." I can feel myself traveling there emotionally. "Instead of working through it, I separated from Duncan and fell into a relationship with another man. I started a marriage with Duncan and then couldn't figure out what my truth was anymore. I just ran away, instead of communicating with him and really trying to work things out. Even if it wouldn't have worked, I'd have liked to have known I gave it my all. He wanted to try and I didn't. I said I did, but the truth is I never really made the effort. He was such a good man and I have a lot of guilt about hurting him and not taking responsibility."

"Have you ever told him that?" he asks. I look at him and see there is no judgment.

"No. I hope some day I can."

Sharing our lives becomes effortless. A safe space is created between us. Each day opens up more opportunities for vulnerability. He asks me questions he genuinely wants to know the answers to, and he listens carefully. He scratches my back at night while we talk and he plays romantic songs for me after hard discussions. I can feel my emotions deepening and I have no desire to fight them.

One night after dinner, Art asks, "Allison, do you think Tanner or Shea will come if we ask them to?" We are driving home on the bumpy old neighborhood road, Vince Gill singing in the background about lost love.

"I don't know, but I think so. I can feel they're around. This whole time I feel like someone has been watching over us, guiding us," I say. Two little Anguillan girls are walking along the narrow road, holding hands. They are barefooted, singing their own tune.

"I agree." There is silence as we pull into the dirt parking area and go upstairs.

I know he wants to know where they are, to feel them, talk with them. He wants what I experienced in the Grand Canyon. I don't know what to do or how to make that happen for him so I decide just to pray that they will come in some way for him.

The next day I get a strong sense that the two boys are in the room. We have just eaten lunch on the balcony and are inside cleaning up. The sun is intense so we are taking a break, relaxing inside. I sit down on the couch.

"Art . . . they're here." I try not to overreact or let him feel my excitement. I'm afraid I'll jinx it.

Art sits still for a while, trying desperately to feel what I am experiencing. Finally he says, "I can't feel them. What is it like?"

"I can't describe it, really. Maybe like having a light blanket draped over your body," I say. We sit there for a minute, me trying to will them into him. I want this for him and feel myself almost calling out to them in my heart.

All of a sudden an empty Coke can next to Art on the glass coffee table begins to move. We both watch it and look at one another.

A message comes into my mind, a voice. "Art, watch the can. They are playing a game with you." I can feel both Tanner and Shea laughing. I smile at their game.

Art picks up the Coke can to check for condensation. It's completely dry. He puts the can down and it moves again.

"They need to see you smile. This is so fun for them. They want to play with you." I pause and try to hear what the "voice" is telling me. "It's hard for them to endure your pain as well as their own. They miss you so much. They miss the joy, the love they had with you."

A big smile begins to break over Art's face along with the tears. They are really here.

A few nights later we are lying on the bed talking after dinner and a late walk on the beach. I am on my side, my cheek resting against my bicep. I am content after a good meal and long walk.

"You up for a game of cribbage?" Art asks.

"Hmm?" I look at him but almost see right through him. I am in a daze, my eyes only partly in focus. The tingling is beginning.

"Hey? Where'd you go? You never say no to cards."

"Art. Lie down on your back and close your eyes. I'm feeling them again—stronger this time." There are voices; it seems they are saying things I can't quite hear. "Just lie there and think of them." All I can think of to do in order to get them closer to Art is to pray silently.

After a few minutes I stop praying. I can sense something will happen. Voices become clear. "Can he feel us? Does he know we are here? I want him to feel me touching him." The two boys' voices are simultaneous. "I miss him. Tell him I miss him—I want to be there." I touch Art's hand to hold it. My eyes are closed in order to concentrate, but I relay each thing said to him. "Ask him if he remembers camping. Lake Powell? I was on his shoulders a lot. He knows I like to be close to him."

"Yes," Art says, "this is Shea." Tears come as he squeezes my hand. "Please tell him I miss him so much. Desperately."

Messages go back and forth. Some are given to me in pictures, others in words. "Art, they are on your chest. They want to be close to your heart. Shea says, 'Where he will always be.' " I open my eyes and can see them lying all over him. Though the vision isn't strong I can see both of them and I'm able to show Art where each is positioned on him. I can't touch them nor do I try to. I simply outline them for their dad, who by now is weeping. He wraps his arms around where they are, holding them in the only way he can now. I see him stroking their heads and rubbing his fingers down their spines. All three are smiling and crying at once. I watch in silence, curled in a ball, allowing the sadness and joy to permeate me as well. Time stops and I do nothing to break its spell. Much later, the two boys begin to move.

I ask if there is anything they want to tell their dad. I ask in my mind, not out loud. They answer similarly, "Tell him we're good . . . we're in a great place. We miss him . . . but we're happy there. We'll be together but much later." There's a hesitation. Without asking I understand there's conflict. They are lonely without him. They stretch out their arms wide to show the pain, the emptiness they have without him. The longing they feel is shown in pictures, many of which I have no comprehension of. I can't understand that kind of love yet. "We will wait. We will wait for him."

This place, this heaven, for lack of a better word, is a place they are happy to be until they can be together again. Tanner is definitely where Shea is now. He is no longer staying back to protect his dad as he was before in the canyon. Their bond—the bond between a father and child—will only strengthen and grow. A picture is given to me for Art. There's a shrine or sacred place where a symbol of the love all three share is placed. It's a place they can visit and stay to connect with him, help him. It is near where they are. I see it amid white light, with gold light surrounding it. This space will remain protected until he joins them. Then it will be gifted to others who need it.

Art says, tears streaming down his face, "Tell them I love them more than ever, that I loved being with them. I don't want them to leave." There is pleading in his voice. "I don't understand why all this had to happen to our life together, but they will always be my boys. Tell them I miss them . . . so badly." He is dissolved, as am I.

Shea and Tanner's eyes look into mine. It's time for them to go and Art can feel the shift. They wash me with emotion, thanking me. I lie down next to Art and hold him the rest of the night.

"We leave in three days. I don't want this to end," Art says. We are lying on the bed much like the night Shea and Tanner visited. They haven't come again. I look into Art's eyes, thinking of all that has transpired over the past two weeks,

"I don't either. I'm falling in love with you. I don't want to go back to the real world." This discussion creeps up as we both are testing the waters to see what our next step is.

"I'd like you to consider moving back to Aspen. I'm established there with my law practice so I really can't leave. What would you think of that, moving back?"

"I hated the winter. And the truth is, it isn't what I'd

have picked. I'm a southern girl. But I want to be with you. I want this and I don't want to do it long distance."

"I don't either."

The overhead fan makes a funny noise so I reach up and pull the string, increasing the power. I lie back down, allowing the air to cool my burned skin.

"How about this?" I say. "I'll move back and we'll do a six-month trial and we'll go from there."

"That's a good plan. You won't be leaving," he says with a smile. I attempt to push him off the bed, daring him to prove it.

A few nights later, our last on the island, we take the conversation deeper. The dance of courtship speeds up. The empty days filled with quiet intimacy have allowed intense feelings to surface. Art would rather the silence be our intimacy; for me it comes with words, lots of them. We compromise, but the words come more often than not. I have talked with him about every aspect of my life, every dream and desire. Tonight the subject is children, something my passions— and his—run high on.

"I've had a vasectomy. I'll have to get it reversed. It may not even work," Art says.

"Are you open to adoption if it doesn't?" Though I want children from my own belly, I am not opposed to the idea. I know I can fully love any child.

"I would be okay with adoption. Let me look into a reversal first and we'll go from there."

"How many do you want?" I ask nervously.

"Two." I can tell this is important to him. "I'm older and I don't know how much energy I'd have for more than that."

"I could have more. But two's okay. How about two boys?" I smile as I see his eyes well up with tears. We are silent for a moment, each dreaming.

"*That* would be amazing. But I love girls, too," he says.

"Me, too. I always wanted girls. Now I think I'd like to have two boys." I smile again, some part of me wondering, almost knowing. We stretch our legs out onto the coffee table where the empty Coke can still sits, a reminder, a calling to believe. The sliding glass door looking out onto the beach is open and the tide is coming in. The ceiling fan hums and I close my eyes, listening to its tune. Art plays with my fingers and I can feel him thinking about these things.

"I can't imagine the chance to be a dad again. To have another child. What if we did have two boys?" There is a pause, a catch in his voice. Every word he says feels more pronounced with my eyes closed. "I'd have to believe in miracles."

As I close my eyes again that night to go to sleep I think back to our conversation and wonder if I really believe it can all happen. The feelings are coming so quickly, so strongly, I have to wonder if it's too crazy. I lie still and check in with my heart. There is nothing but hope.

Calling All Angels

ALLISON AND I PART WAYS IN MIAMI, AND ON MY FLIGHT back to Denver I think back on all that happened on the island. It's my first chance to process the whole experience without Allison around. We've been together two weeks, and I realize that I am now at peace with welcoming someone new into my life. Of course, part of me realizes the danger here. I know I have fallen in love with Allison, but I ask myself whether I feel this way because of her amazing connection to my family—particularly the boys—and the way she has allowed me to feel ever more connected to them myself. We are all enmeshed—Allison, Tanner, Shea, Kathy, and me. Allison and I both have questions about how that will work out, but we both want to find the answers. What I do know is that I love her spirit, her compassion, and her openness to life.

With Allison on Anguilla, for the first time, really, I felt the boys close to me and I knew their words. It wasn't just wishing and wanting them to be there that caused the dry Coke can to move across that glass table. It just happened, and there is no other explanation for it. And when Allison started feeling their presence again a few nights later and we relayed our thoughts and feelings to each other, I began to realize that Allison is the boys'—and maybe even Kathy's—gift to me. While I miss their physical presence as much, if not more, a part of my soul is filled with a peace and thankfulness that they are right there reaching out. There is a faith—in them, their everlasting love—that somehow has lodged itself inside of me. I can't pretend to fully understand it, but as I arrive back to Aspen and to our empty home, I find myself believing they are with me, feeling everything I am. This faith wraps around me and comforts the ache. It is also nice to feel certain of their presence, which somehow seems to free me to delight in my growing feelings for Allison and to trust in those feelings. Knowing their intimate part in it all, I no longer feel any hesitancy, any doubt, about what is right. We are moving into this new love together, in shared joy and hope.

Bless this girl, she actually does it. She quits the job in Dallas before she even begins it; she packs up her stuff in Austin and moves back to Aspen to be with me. Outside of work we spend all of our time together. Allison is eager to try new things, and I have a lot of fun teaching her what I know. I begin introducing her to my favorite summer and fall activities. I get her a mountain bike and a pair of Rollerblades, and on weekends we hike the endless high trails and I take her to places that are sacred to me. We go deep into the Hunter Creek Valley and I tell her about the role that it played in Aspen's mining days, with the hunters and the homesteaders and the toll road and the mines and shafts and the great ore tunnels beneath the valley floor. She's fascinated with the remnants of the Electric Light Dam, more than a mile up the valley. I tell her it once held a reservoir that fed a long flume that eventually dropped into a pair of turbines in a building that is now the Aspen Art Museum, providing electricity for the entire mining town. Through Allison's eyes and experiences, I rediscover this town that I hold so close to my heart.

Although I am still filled with raw emotions that are close to the surface, I'm gradually learning how to ride this seesaw of despair and joy. I know that I've fallen in love with Allison, and each day it seems that I have a little more to give of myself to her and to Piper and to others close to me. Increasingly I find myself allowing, even reaching for, the times when I can genuinely smile. Yet the pain, the missing, the longing for my lost family never leave me, and they never will.

The ache is so intense that when I search my body to try to find where it is lodged, it seems that it is everywhere in me, that every cell in my body yearns for them to come home so that we can be complete once again. We were so fine together. The boys filled me with a light and love that I'd never known before, and I don't know if I will ever be that whole again. As my new relationship grows, and as life begins again to take on color and purpose, I remain committed to honoring myself and my family in all that I do. Their love for me, their place in my life and in my heart, gave me so much of the strength and compassion and joy of living that I have today. Every fiber of me embraces and remembers them. And though I am not yet fully conscious of it, Kathy and Shea and Tanner are still breathing life and hope into me, and they are helping me find out who I have become.

There are still nights that we stay up until all hours while I tell Allison stories about the boys. She wants to hear them all, so that she can understand the love that we shared. She lies there stroking my head, wiping my tears or laughing with me about our adventures.

Allison and I struggle to find a balance for ourselves, for our different wants and needs. While this being in love is a wondrous thing, we both realize that I have a lot of grieving to do alone. There are many times when we can share the pain and she can comfort me, but it is important that she not rescue me or become my caretaker. We stumble in these areas, and there are fights and hurt feelings. Slowly we find ways to communicate about these things, to give and take.

"What did I do wrong?" I ask as we walk into the house after a bike ride. We passed two of Kathy's friends on the ride home.

"Nothing," she says. She goes to the kitchen sink to rinse off the breakfast dishes and put them into the dishwasher. Every movement of her body screams anger.

"Nothing? How can you say nothing? You're obviously mad." I turn her around to face me.

"I don't want to talk about it."

"You have to. I know you."

"Do you really want to know?" she asks.

"Yes," I say.

"Okay," she says. The anger changes to hurt and the tears spill out. "It's hard. Everything is about them. Everything. People stare at me, wondering what my intentions are. People talk about your family all the time." She blows her nose and then leans her forehead onto mine. "And I live with a man who cares about me but spends all of his time missing his family. It hurts. I hurt. Living with it, watching you, feeling your pain is hard." I hold her while she cries.

"What can I do?" I ask.

"Nothing. That's just it. You have your journey in all of this. And I have mine."

"I don't think that's the whole story, Alf. I think we need to find ways for you and me to separate from them at times."

She lifts her head from my shoulder. She has used my shirt as a Kleenex. She smiles and says, "I like that idea."

Hard Times

Though I had the visions of Tanner and Shea in the Grand Canyon and on Anguilla, once I get to Aspen I don't feel them as much as I do Kathy. I think that my heart has shifted to grief for the boys; every time I look at their images and see who they were through the pictures, I am saddened even more that they have died. When I was in the Grand Canyon, I knew very little about them.

Kathy has made her presence felt since I have come to live in the house. Her artwork and photography cover the walls. Haitian art was her favorite and several pieces that she and Art brought back from the islands are striking. But I find myself staring at her own versions of Haitian art, bright colors that surround black women in some Caribbean marketplace. While hers resembles the Haitian artists' work, it is distinctly her own. Her photos tell me two things about her—she could draw people into her lens and make them feel comfortable with themselves in the moment. It is evident from the pictures of her boys that they invited her into the very special love that ran deep between the two of them.

I can't remember a first time when I knew she was around. She was just there. Then, when I was feeling mad, I would begin to feel her presence strongly, almost as if she would jump out of her artwork and be in the room. I rarely see her; I only hear her voice when I quiet my mind. At first it is unsettling because our talks are sometimes heated owing to our strong personalities, and later I realize she is only trying to help me, so I welcome her.

"Kathy, I can't stand him right now. I don't know why I am here. I don't even know if this is going to work out or not." Pent up anger is seething. Art has said something over the phone that hurt my feelings. I am in the yard weeding the flower bed that surrounds the monster tree in our front yard. Sun shines into my eyes when I look up and around to make sure no neighbor is listening. Part of me wants to go inside the house and get my sunglasses; part of me is afraid if I do I'll get distracted and the conversation will be over.

"You know exactly why you're here, Allison. Get over it. You signed on for this. This is about you, not him. You have skated through life, controlling every man in every relationship. You need to grow up. It's time." Her voice is calm, which angers me even more.

"What right do you have to say that? How do you know any of this? How do I know this is all real?"

"I'm telling you the truth, aren't I?" When I don't

respond, she continues. "It's called a gut check. You have everything it takes to be the woman you know you can be. Instead you haven't pushed yourself to grow, to find out what you are really made of." She is firm but loving. The gut check is working.

"Who is that woman? Who am I? I don't know why I am here or what all that means."

"That's it! You got it," Kathy replies.

"What?"

"Think about it. Just sit with it." Her voice is still.

I walk around the yard and finally decide to sit down in the hammock. I'm tired of pacing. It's a beautiful fall day. The mountains have snow on their crests; the leaves are orange and brown, just beginning to come down. I am in the middle of a conversation with my future husband's dead wife. I laugh to myself. "Get a life," I think. I get up and look for a nice place to sit on the ground. There is a need to be close to the earth. All the neighbors are probably looking from their kitchen windows and see me talking to the air. If so, they must wonder if I need to be committed. I wonder, too. I finally lie down on the ground and look up. I close my eyes to shut out the sun. I begin to pray. My heart cracks open and I start to bleed—loneliness, sorrow, insecurity, self-hatred. I curl up in a ball, the autumn leaves sticking to my clothes. They are a blanket, a cushion to the pain coming out. "God, where are you? What do you want from me? Do you really love me?"

I stay there, fetal-like, for what seems like a long time. I let all the tears come that will and finally I feel peace come over me like an anesthesia. I am half in my body, half floating. It is as if I am a balloon high up in the sky that has been popped and the balloon has spiraled all over, left and right, flailing rapidly until finally the source of its survival is emptied from its body. Oddly, it is a relief, a panacea. I think of my favorite childhood story—*The Velveteen Rabbit*. I am that rabbit—all worn and beat up, the stuffing taken out. I know I am worth loving, that I have a lot to give, but I don't know who will want me.

I can feel Kathy come back. She must have drifted for a while. She is kneeling next to me. I still can't see her but her presence is so strong I have no doubt she is there. I liken it to feeling the wind or a raindrop—to describe the sensation is almost impossible, but the specific feelings associated with it are obvious. "Now you see, don't you?" she says quietly, almost a whisper.

"Not really. I must be a slow learner." She laughs at this.

"You surrendered. Just for that moment. You gave in. You stopped being the superwoman you think you should be. This is all about you and nothing to do with you. You talked to your God and let him in."

"I'm not very happy with him either right now. I don't even know who he or she is," I say.

"I know. And that is where you start . . . with the 'not knowing' and the humility to just find out who you are in the pain . . . to sit with the 'experience' of that pain. Do you think we find ourselves in joy? We may appreciate ourselves in the good times and be thankful for that time because it feels good inside. But we really find ourselves—the guts—in the shit, in the pain. We find out who we are, what we can be and what we are made of. We can't do any of that until we surrender and admit that we are not the ones in control."

I sit with that for a while. It fits my soul like a glove. I don't want to hear it, but I know it resonates within me. I have lived a life filled with pain as well as joy.

Memories come back, haunting me; times when I failed or was rejected surface in my mind.

"It's the same fear, Allison," Kathy says, not wanting to break the spell of my memory.

"I thought I was all done with that," I say.

"Nice try." She laughs with me. "But this time there's another twist to it. It goes even deeper."

"You mean with Art?"

"Intimacy. Having to bear it all. Deciding to let go of all of those walls you have carefully built up," she says.

"This hurts." I feel warm tears hit my cheek. "Art's pain scares me."

"As it should. But let me give you a little piece of advice I never got—or at least I never was able to push through in my own life and practice with Art." I can hear her regret. I understand there is no threat, that there is no agenda in this conversation. She is here, befriending me, out of love and to give me a gift she has never given herself. She can help me, someone very similar to her in many ways, to grow and make changes she never was able to make. As she continues to communicate in my mind, the deepest part of me opens to hear her. This is as much for her as for me. "Just let go. Stop trying to hold on. Look him in the eyes and put yourself out there. You are afraid he won't stay if he knows you. The opposite is true. Your fear is about not ever being good enough. You have tried to please everyone your whole life, just to feel their love." There is a pause. "Just love you. It's time for you to find out who you are . . . the truth. Then you need to take that woman and share her with Art. She may not be sweet, loving, and perfect all the time. That needs to be okay with you and those you trust. Allison, it's about getting honest for the first time in your life and then sharing that honesty with another."

I am anxious already. "What happens if Art can't handle me? I don't know if anyone can. There's a lot in there and it's pretty complicated."

She sits with the question. "That has to be okay. You have to know that you can't control other people and you have to be able to accept that not everyone may be able to handle the real you."

"Oh, great. And that's supposed to comfort me?"

"No, no it's not. But it's honest—and that is what you want." There is a shift in her; a softness I can almost touch comes through. "I will tell you that Art will think it is beautiful. He is ready for you. He may not always understand it, but he is there in his own life. He is able to see you and love you."

Thus began my dialogue with Kathy. As our communicating continues, I realize that I have never before felt so safe with another woman. I find myself feeling stronger for having been with her. Maybe because there is a constant questioning in my mind—that I am "talking" with her—but I find myself letting go of any doubts and just enjoy being with her. I am totally myself instead of trying to say the right thing. When masks are set aside, so much vulnerability comes out. I love her sense of self. I find it enables me to find my own. With Kathy I feel I have a true friend.

Moving on Together

FROM THE FIRST, ALLISON TELLS ME ALL ABOUT HER TALKS
with Kathy. In some ways it is a bit strange, but strange has
become a part of my life ever since Allison's first experience
on the Tanner Trail. Mostly it is amazing—and comforting
for both me and Allison. Kathy talks to Allison and uses
phrases the way she did when she was alive. Of course, it com-
plicates things for me emotionally in that I love Allison and
here she is talking with my late wife. What I love most is the
blessing I feel from Kathy. It dispels any lingering doubts
about taking the next step with Allison.

Mostly now I'm focusing on an important practical matter. As winter approaches I begin searching for an experienced urologist. I want to marry Allison and to try to create
a family together, but I'm worried about whether the reversal
will be successful after six years of being tied off, and I don't
know for sure that I'll be fertile even if it works. She says she
is open to adoption, and I could be happy with that, too, but

we both want to have our own children if it is at all possible. I want the operation to be performed by the finest surgeon available.

A woman I know who runs a ski program for young children at Buttermilk Mountain tells me about a Dr. Ning, who has participated with her for many years in an annual medical mission to poor villages in the mountains of Vietnam. He's apparently one of the top urologists in the country, he practices out of Denver, and she says she'll put me in touch with him. The next day she calls back with a phone number, and I place the call right away.

"Art, thank you for calling me," Dr. Ning says. "I know of you and the loss of your family. I saw it on the news channels and I have thought about you many times."

"I know of your reputation, and I'd like you to perform my surgery," I say. "I'd like you to help me have another chance to have children."

"I'd give anything for that opportunity," he replies. "My problem is, I've just retired. I would be willing to come out of retirement for this—and I looked into it when I heard you might call. But there is no way for me to reactivate my insurance to perform a single surgery. I'm sorry about that."

My heart sinks. He's the best, and I was counting on him.

"I have a great idea, though," he continues. "I trained a very fine surgeon in Denver named Randall Meachum. He's as good as I ever was, maybe even better. I'm going to call him and tell him about you, and you can set things up with his office." We talk a little longer, and he helps me with some of my layman's questions about the procedure. As we close the conversation, he says, "Art, I wish you the very best. I really want this to work for you."

I thank him for his kindness and his time, and I tell him that I'll wait a day or two to call Dr. Meachum. Dr. Ning's personal concern for me and his desire to help have touched me.

As I hang up the phone and sit in my office I feel how fast my heart is beating. I realize that I'm scared—that the operation will fail, that something won't work right. I'm afraid of disappointing Allison. A part of me wonders what she'll do if we can't have children. As I sit there with it, though, I begin to understand that my greatest fear is personal: it's about me and my own dreams. I want this to happen so very, very much. I want to be a dad again, to help a child grow and become all that he or she can be. I want to be a part of that eternal connection again, that finest school, the love between a parent and a child. Dear God, help me to become a father again.

Dr. Meachum meets with me the following week, and we schedule the surgery for just before Christmas, his first available opening. His entire office is warm and accommodating, and I realize how much he and all the nurses and staff want this operation to be successful. The surgery goes smoothly, and after waiting two long months we go back to Denver for testing to find out what's happening in my body. I provide a sperm sample, and the nurse places it under a microscope.

Dr. Meachum comes into the room, studies the lens, and then turns it over to me with a smile. There are thousands of sperm swimming and darting in every direction, and he tells us that we couldn't have hoped for a better result. Allison spends a few minutes gazing into the microscope, and then looks up at me with a silly grin and we hug each other tightly, tears streaming down our faces. Dr. Meachum encourages us to get busy trying to have a baby because scar tissue can build up where the tube was reconnected.

The next several months are filled with hopes and expectations and disappointments and the frustrations of two people wanting things badly and not communicating very well about what they are feeling. Secretly, I am planning to ask Allison to marry me on Easter Sunday, but she's apparently about had it with the waiting. We have a big fight the night before, and on Easter morning there's a ten-page letter waiting for me on the bathroom counter. I figure that instead of reading the letter, I'd better get on with my plan. I wake Allison with a cup of coffee and when she seems reasonably alert I ask her if she'll be my wife. Thankfully, she says yes, she would love that. After all, that is what the fight and the letter were about, although perhaps not in those exact words. Allison is ready for this. She's spent the past year with me, she's grieved for me and with me, and she's done all the "firsts"—the first Christmas without them, their birthdays, the anniversary of their deaths. She doesn't want to leave them behind in any way, but she knows now that we have a chance to create our own life, our own family. It's her turn.

That day, as we hold one another and pledge to get married later in the spring on a lonely beach on a far island, we also conceive a child. We don't know yet about this new life, but in the years ahead we will have our own special reasons for celebrating the Resurrection.

The Herald Angel

Born that man no more may die,
Born to raise the sons of earth
Born to give them second birth
Hark, the herald angels sing.

I wake up startled. I rub my eyes, adjusting to the morning light. Looking around the room, I remind myself I'm back in Texas visiting my family and friends. It's about a month after Easter. I lie back down and pull an extra pillow over my head, attempting to go back to sleep. The dream resurfaces in my mind and I can see it even clearer than in sleep.

I'm standing alone in a long, seemingly endless room. The ceilings are far away and only by the change in shades of blue can I tell which way is up. I look around, wondering where I am and why I'm here. Deep blue, a mixture of aqua and azure, surrounds me. I feel like I'm floating and for a second I wonder if I'm a part of the sky. There are no doors or windows, no way for me to leave. Oddly, I'm not afraid. Instead, I feel a deep sense of weightlessness, of peace. The wondrous blue becomes a mood within me, a feeling I can literally touch.

Out of the corner of my eye I see movement and before I dare to look I know it's a child. The space it takes up is small and the energy it gives off is gentle. I turn and recognize Shea sitting on the ground looking at me, waiting. Part of me wants to run to him, part of me holds back. I look at him, asking with my eyes what I should do. His expression tells me to wait.

He stands up and walks closer to me, holding something in his arms that I'm unable to see clearly. Time seems to slow down as tears spring into my eyes. He is so small, still so full of "child" inside. Knowing how much Art misses him makes me wish Art were here, not me. Shea's steps are slow, full of purpose. Ten feet away he stops. His face is turned slightly down as his eyes look up and into mine. Deep pools of brown, looking through me with a perfect innocence that breaks my heart. He wants nothing from me and yet everything. In that minute I want to live up to everything he is asking of me. I tell him I will do anything for him.

Everything changes. His body begins to lift up, to fly, and his arms open up toward me, a smile so bright on his face. His head flings back in joy as laughter fills the air. He flies toward me. Something is released from his arms and I reach out to catch it. I smile back, trying to touch him, to capture his joy. I can't get any closer and I can tell he is leaving me. He has delivered his message, performed his mission of love, and his untamed spirit is soaring once again.

I take the pillow off my face, raw with emotion. The dream is gone but the vision, the clarity, and preciseness of it will be printed on my heart forever. I go into the bathroom and splash water on my face. What is it that Shea was giving to me? I stare at myself in the mirror. I don't feel very stable on my feet so I go back and lie down. I look around the room—Rod's old room that I can't seem to stop myself from sleeping in every time I come home—and realize I'd better start packing. I'm flying back home to Aspen today.

Turbulence hits the airplane between Denver and Aspen. It feels like a roller coaster. I keep a wary eye on the barf bag. I warn the man sitting next to me and he quickly moves to another seat under the scolding stare of the flight attendant in the front of the plane. I pull the bag out and open it to the ready position, when suddenly the turbulence is over. I'm sweating, and I take deep breaths to calm myself down.

As the plane approaches Aspen I look out to the lightly snow-capped mountains below, and I'm drawn to the blueness of the sky. The purity of the color takes me back to my dream. As we touch down, the pieces of the puzzle fall together within me and I'm suddenly tingling with excitement. I ask my friend Laura, who is picking me up, to stop by the drugstore on the way home. I may have a surprise for Art.

"Hi, Alf. How was the trip home?" Art asks as he walks in from work and gives me a sweet kiss. I'm cooking our dinner in the kitchen. I stop to kiss him back and look into his face. The one-year anniversary of the accident is several months past now, but his eyes still reflect an intense longing. I want to give him something to bring happiness back to those eyes.

"Good. You got my message?" I can't stop smiling as I continue cooking.

"Yeah. Sorry. Meetings all day." He chews on a cracker and cheese. He looks a little tired. "I'm glad you're back."

"I have a surprise for you," I say, and I point to the small box and card that are sitting on the counter. I am bursting. "Please open them."

I turn the stove down and come to lean next to him. He opens the card. It's a baby card and there's a cute baby hat in the box.

"Are you sure? This is for real?" His face says more than words. Tears of joy, not pain, appear in his eyes. "We're going to have a baby?"

"Yes . . . Yes!" I show him the pregnancy test. Then I tell him about the dream. "It just hit me on the plane, Art, that Shea was giving me a precious gift for you."

The Mystery of Hope

THE DAY HAS COME. ALL MY TEARS AND PAIN AND PRAYERS and hopes are met in this moment, and once again I am waiting for God. Allison is lying on a bed in the birthing room, her face red and her hair wet with sweat. Piper and I are standing on either side of her doing our best to give her the love she needs. Piper has been with me before in this, and when our eyes meet we share our unspoken awe and wonder that we have come to be here again. It's been twelve hours since they began to induce Allison's labor, but after a strong epidural, a couple of naps, and some mellow music, she's a lot more comfortable than she was earlier. "Push . . . come on, Allison . . . just one more and you can rest again." Linda, the midwife who has assisted Allison throughout the pregnancy, continues to encourage her as the birth draws close. Linda has a son who played on Tanner's hockey team, and she wants this child born safely. She wants new life for me, too.

"The head is coming now, Allison. Start your breathing exercise again and we'll give another big push." The top of the head appears, and Linda says, "Art, it's almost time. Come on down here. I want you to help me pull this baby out." There are tears in her eyes.

Grief has held me in its grip for twenty-two months now, and I can literally feel it beginning to lift away. I think of the emperor penguins and the relief they must feel when spring arrives and the excruciating mating march to and from the sea in eighty-below-zero winter storms finally comes to an end. Once again they have brought a baby penguin into the world and nourished it through the fragile early days. The harsh ritual is thousands of years old, and they have survived it. Not all do. As I move to the foot of the bed I realize that I, too, have survived one of life's terrible storms, and that I am ready to hold my new child. I'm going to be a father again.

Rider slides smoothly out of his mother into my hands. The last time I held a son, he was leaving this world; now I am bringing one into life. There is a sudden radiance about us, and I wonder if angels come to dance and sing in the presence of miracles. I am filled with an overwhelming sense of gratitude, and I want this profound and perfect time to last forever. I look into Rider's tiny face as he yells out his first breath, proclaiming his arrival, and I say to him almost silently, "Rider-man, oh how much I'm going to love you, we are going to do the finest things together. Thank you for coming to me." I hand him to Linda for a wipe down, and I reach up and cut the umbilical cord. Linda tucks the baby into Allison's arms.

I lean over to kiss Allison and I tell her how much I love her. Tears cloud her vision as she hands our new son back to me. She wants him in my arms. He is a gift for both of us, but in this magical moment Rider is her gift to me. Everything inside me is dancing.

When Rider was growing inside her she could feel the kind of child he was going to be. Driving through Glenwood Canyon one day after meeting a friend in Vail, Rider began to kick her hard and do somersaults in her belly. She called me at my office on her cell phone and described where she was in the canyon. I told her she had just passed through the accident site. The child, of course, knew exactly where they were. And at night when I would snuggle up next to Allison in bed, Rider would move to be as close to me as possible.

I look at Allison and then at Piper and realize that the whole room is silent. It is filled with pure joy. Even if I could speak, which I don't seem able to do, I couldn't begin to describe everything that I'm feeling. After the nurses check all of his vital signs and weigh him, Piper and I quietly give Rider his first warm bath. He's such a beautiful child.

Welcome to the World

I am exhausted but overjoyed. Art and I have brought new life into this world together. As Art cradles Rider in his arms, I feel the presence of Tanner and Shea and Kathy in the room with us, in a space just beyond perception. I look at Art and can tell by his expression that he senses what is happening to me. Of course they have come. The boys have been waiting patiently for this day, to be with their father who has remained so much a part of them. The hospital cannot be an easy place for them. It is painfully reminiscent. Within these pale walls, with doctors and nurses in the halls, they can feel death as strongly as they can life. In a hospital not far from here, their own physical bodies gave way and were left behind. Loneliness lingers in these memories. Yet this is a different time and space, those wounds are healing, and they are here to be with their father—and with me. They're here to see darkness turn to light, to witness the magic of hope.

They watch silently, holding hands. They smile with joy, tears streaming down their faces. They can feel their father's powerful emotions, and they are profoundly thankful that he has a new child, another boy. Each of them in their own way helped form this child. He is given to this world, and especially to their father, for special reasons. Like all children, he will be a great blessing, but he will also be a reflection. In looks and emotions he will be uncannily like Tanner. This boy will be a truth teller and will see into the souls of others. It will not always be easy for him.

As Shea and Tanner look on, witnessing the scene, they sense that they will soon be moving on to a higher place. Tanner looks to Kathy and asks, "Mom, will it mean that we won't be as close?" He is afraid of losing the connection. "Will Dad still miss us?"

"Sweet baby," Kathy responds, "you will never lose that. At times he will think of you even more often, because this boy will be so much like you. He is filled with joy to have a new son, but he wishes you both were there, too, and that feeling will never leave him. And he knows deep inside that when his time there is done he will be coming home to you, and that is part of his dream." She pauses and looks down at Art. "Do you see the touch of sadness still in his eyes? It will always be there. He is thinking of you, remembering when you were born. You were perfect, too."

When Rider is three months old, I have an operation to repair an old injury that caused my shoulder to dislocate about a dozen times while I was pregnant. The anesthetic causes my breast milk to dry up. One night a month later Tanner comes to me in almost the same dream that Shea did in Texas, giddy with expectation. He has a secret for me, a gift, and once again I can't quite make it out. When I wake in the morning I look over at Art and whisper, "I need to take a pregnancy test. I think I'm pregnant again."

"What do you mean?" he says. "It isn't possible." We've barely had any sex, owing to the pain and complications with my shoulder.

"Tanner came to me last night in a dream and gave me something, just the way Shea did when I was pregnant with Rider. I know what it means, Art." My husband looks at me quizzically. We both know the odds are against it.

Art heads off to work. An hour later, Rider and I arrive at his office with a positive pregnancy test and some balloons to celebrate. Art sits silently looking at me, his eyes moist. He can't quite believe it, but I can feel the joy beginning to grow within him. A big smile breaks out on his face. He's going to have another child. It's everything that he has prayed for, but he never thought it would happen so soon. I already know it's a boy.

Blessed Again

THE BIRTH OF A CHILD. ALL OF THE HOPES OF MANKIND BEGIN here, and nowhere is God more present. I catch Burke as he enters the world, cut his cord, and hold him up to his mother. I am struck by the aura of peacefulness that seems to surround him. He is ready for this world, he belongs here. He will be a wild one, blessed with great physical skills, but he will some day be a healer. I cannot say that I know these things yet, but there is something that allows me a glimpse of who our young boy will be. Rider is already deeply connected to him. He constantly touched him in his mother's belly, a smile glowing on his little face. They are very different souls, but they will be as close as two brothers can be.

Seeing Tanner

I walk into the boys' bathroom and fill up the little red cup with water. It's a nightly ritual. Rider, I know, will be asking for it since I forgot to bring it in when I scratched his back a few minutes ago. Burke is already fast asleep, sprawled out against the protective netting on the top bunk. He decided years ago that the top bunk is where he wanted to make his home. Thank God for the netting. Burke, who pushes all limits in life, would fall out every night without it. Rider is happy to be safe and secure in the bottom bunk.

I realize I have drifted off into space in my being-a-mom exhaustion and that water is pouring all over my hands while it overflows the cup. I touch the silver C nozzle for cold and turn it off. As I dry my hands I remember that earlier today I was thinking of how so many letters have words that coincide. C and see, B and bee, O and oh, P and pee. Having children and trying to explain the English language puts a whole new light on words and what they mean.

"Mom. *Mom.*" I am drying the outside of the cup.

"I'm coming. I've got your water, Rider."

"No. Mom. Go get Dad. Now."

Generally Rider doesn't talk to me like this. He's insistent, commanding, even alarmed. I don't allow what I call smart talk, but I can tell there is something going on. I put the water down on the dresser. "What's up?"

"Mom. Please go get Dad." He is looking off, toward the window. His eyes won't leave the spot where he is staring. "Tanner is in the window, Mom, and I'm afraid he'll leave."

I race downstairs and find Art in the kitchen cleaning up. "You need to go upstairs now. Rider needs you." I want Rider to be the one to tell him. "It's really important."

"I'll go in a sec. I want to finish up here."

"No, Art. Go." I can't tell if he'll hurry. "Rider is seeing Tanner."

"What?" He throws down the towel he is wiping the counter with and races up the stairs two at a time. I follow him, unsure if it is okay for me to be a part of this. I want this for the two of them. Three of them, really. I'm with our boys so much and I've also been the one to have the experiences with Art's other family. I want this moment, this intimate time with the merging of two sets of sons, to happen just with Art.

I perch myself on the step outside the boys' room. I hear the sound of their voices. I hear none of the words, only the rhythm. I am hypnotized by it. I lie down and curl up on the carpet at the top of the stairs and wonder what is being said.

Finally, Art comes out, smiles at me, takes my hand, and leads me down the hall to our bedroom. "What did he say?" I ask. "Was Tanner still there?"

"Hang on. I'll tell you everything. We just had the most amazing talk." We sit down on the bed and I curl my knees to my chest. I have chills. My eyeballs feel as if they are popping out of my head.

"When I walked in he said Tanner wasn't really there anymore but that he had been and he was still around but he couldn't see him as clearly." Art pauses and sits back against the headboard of our bed. "Tanner had been there to let him know that he is his angel and that he watches over him and Burke. He wanted Rider to know that he was his brother and his friend, that he would protect him, take care of him."

I sit there and readjust my body, dying to hear more. "Tanner wanted me to know that they were 'doing good' as Rider put it, that they were together and happy." There are tears in his eyes. "Rider said Tanner misses me." The tears fall and I reach over to touch his arm. "Allison, it was so beautiful. It was such a gift. And the amazing thing is that Rider got it. I mean he wasn't freaked out at all. He just wanted me to see Tanner, too. He's totally fine with the whole thing."

I'm not surprised. This is the child who at the age of one carried Tanner and Shea's pictures around the house with him, kissing them. Neither Art nor I had mentioned who they were yet. He was only a baby. He already knew them. He loved them even then.

"Could you feel anything?" I ask. "Did it feel like Tanner was there?"

"I don't know what this means, really . . ." He pauses and thinks. "The room was still. And quiet. And there was an electric feeling in the air like when you were young and someone shocked you after rubbing their feet on the carpet."

"I love that."

We sit in silence for a while, him examining his experience, me relishing in his joy.

"I just can't believe he had such a clear vision of Tanner," I say.

"It seemed authentic. He wasn't making it up."

"I love this, Art. I love it that they are visiting us and that our boys will know them in this way."

Art gets up to wash his face. We are so different, I think. I can't move, my body is humming and I want to talk about every word, every detail. He needs to process what happened, to experience the truth of it. After a while he continues. "Rider and I had this great talk about my love for Tanner and Shea and how much I love him and Burke. I told him that he and Burke are so important to me . . . that they have given me back my hope and my faith. You know what he said? You're not going to believe this, Allison."

"What?" I lean back against the headboard, fluffing up a pillow. The night is cool and the windows in our room are open so I pull the comforter over my body. "He said Tanner and Shea were a part of picking them to come and be with me. He said they wanted him and Burke to have the greatest dad." I watch tears flow over his smile. "I don't even know if he understands it. It just came out of his mouth. He looked at me sort of surprised at his words. And then he smiled and told me he was so glad he got to be my son. I mean, what's a man supposed to do with that?"

Up on Diamond Head

"Art, I'm taking the boys to water ski."

"Okay. I'll meet you later." He is relaxing.

As dreams go, where nothing makes complete sense, I'm with Rider and Burke on the ocean, taking them out in a speedboat. In the dream I am in a tunnel. All I can see is exactly where I am in the scene, nothing around. It is like looking through a telephoto lens at myself: sometimes I am inside my body; at other times I am an onlooker. The water we are on is blue green, like Anguilla, but we are not there. The water is like glass and the sun is bright; my back feels as though it's beginning to burn.

We're laughing and playing, having fun on the boat. The boys are rough-housing while I drive, enjoying their banter. They decide to Boogie board off the back. We are in a bubble of perfection.

The scene changes and the boat becomes a surfboard with a motor attached. The boys and I are riding on it; it seems perfectly natural for this to have changed. The boys are on the front of the board; I am in the back. All of a sudden there is a big wave and I fall off into the water. The board takes off with them on it. They are six and seven years old and have no idea what to do. They are looking back at me, fearful, reaching their arms out toward me as they did when they were small and wanted to be lifted up into my arms and held. I scream as I see the board disappear, going dangerously fast. There's a knot in my stomach. I know it is not good. They won't know to jump off. I feel as if I'm going to drown in my own hysteria.

All of a sudden I am in the small town near the ocean where we must be visiting. Even in the dream state I feel lost, foreign. I am running down the cobblestone streets near the water, screaming for my babies, begging for someone to help me. In my peripheral vision I see quaint shops and houses. I am trying to figure out where I am, where my boys have gone. I turn to anyone who will listen. "Have you seen my two boys? They are small with very blond hair. They were on a surfboard?"

I continue to run to each small house or business, frantically pleading to anyone who will listen. No one knows, and they go about their lives as if nothing has happened. I wonder if they speak my language. All they do is shake their heads no. Why don't they care? They must feel my terror. I see a police station and begin to go in when I see in the distance a gurney with a child on it. I turn and sprint at full tilt. It seems to take forever to get there. As I run, I'm wondering what I did wrong, what made this happen? Tears are streaming down my face as I run toward my child. I am scared out of my skin as I reach the gurney and look into Burke's face. His face is scraped and torn up almost beyond recognition.

"Burke, it's Mommy. I'm right here, sweetie. Mommy is so sorry. I don't know what happened." My baby. He's so hurt. I want to vomit.

Time stops. He looks at me with his big deep green eyes, and with a purity I have only seen in a child says, "It's okay, Mommy. I'm right here. It's going to be okay." I kiss him and hold him close to my heart. I thank God he is alive. He is taken away from me by nurses and doctors. For some unknown reason I am unable to follow them. My feet are planted and I'm left all alone on the street. There is no one else in sight.

A few minutes later I see another gurney and run toward who I know is Rider. The road seems to go on forever. I feel like I'm running on a treadmill. I can't seem to get to my child. I can't stop sweating and the salt mixes with my tears. I am in a state of shock, moving in my mind toward the realization of what has happened. I'm scared Rider is dead. I think of Art and wonder how I'm going to tell him. He has already lost two boys. How will he handle this? How will I handle this? Will they live? I've been crying, but now am convulsing as I approach. I reach Rider, and he is in the same shape as Burke. Blood covers his swollen face and his arms and legs look broken.

"Oh baby," I say as I lay my head on his chest, touching

his hair. I want to heal him with my will. "Rider, it's Mommy. I'm so sorry. Please talk to me, sweetie. I need you."

He slowly turns his head closer to me and then smiles at me. The moment seems to last forever. "I love you, Mom." He reaches out toward me but is too weak. "Everything is going to be okay. We're not leaving. It's not our time."

He is taken away by the same doctors and nurses and once again I can't move. I collapse, alone, with no one to catch me.

I'm in a cold sweat. I wake up and remember that I'm in a hotel room in Waikiki. I feel as though I have thrown up or am about to. I stumble into the hotel bathroom, put the toilet seat down to sit on, and place my head between my legs. My body aches as if I had run a marathon the day before. In the dark I fumble to turn on the faucet and get a drink of water with my cupped hands, then splash some on my face. "It was only a dream," I tell myself out loud. The taste of bile is still in my mouth. My hair is wet with sweat. I close the bathroom door and feel my way back to the bed I am sharing with Burke. We are on vacation in Hawaii and playing musical beds. Last night was Burke's turn with me. I cuddle up to Burke's soft, warm body. It is still squishy, a touch of baby fat still there. I smell his sweet, morning breath. I listen to his heartbeat and feel his calm breathing. Everything feels important, now that he isn't hurt. I hold him tight, and thank God he is okay, that it was just a dream.

I drift off to the smell of him, never letting myself fully go, for fear of the nightmare returning. Still spooked and nauseous, I do my best to relax. The sun is peeking through the hotel curtains we tried so carefully to close tightly. The air conditioner clicks on and the chilled air feels good against my still wet skin. My body still hasn't recovered. I snuggle up closer to Burke, squeezing him tight. He has been and always will be a healing force in my life.

Later I turn over and glance at the clock—it's 7:30 a.m. I look over at Art and Rider in the bed across from me. Art is awake and waves at me, so as not to wake the boys. I wave back and wonder how to explain the dream. Do I even want to go there with him? I'm still uneasy.

The kids begin to awaken around eight o'clock. "Art, what is the date today?" We have lost count, as we always do on vacation.

"You know, I'm not sure. It's either the twenty-fifth or -sixth." It's February. I can tell he's thinking the same thing I am. "I think it's the twenty-sixth."

"Oh." I realize what day it is for Art, and even for us. "How are you with that?" I ask. Nine years ago today his family was killed. Each year it means more and more to me— Rider, last year, and now Burke is the same age that Shea was when he was killed.

"I'm glad we're here. I'm glad we are all together." It's said with gentleness and certainty. "It's nice to be away from Colorado . . . to be somewhere different."

The kids are now fully awake and going at full tilt. It's

bed jumping and pillow fights with Dad while I shower, then I dress myself and them. There is no time to reflect or get into deep conversations; that will have to wait. In many ways, that's the blessing. These two boys, who give us so much pleasure, give him little time to focus on grief. Their demands are a gift.

We talk briefly at breakfast with Rider and Burke about the anniversary, and we decide to celebrate their lives instead of feeling sadness. We decide to hike up Diamond Head and come back and play in the swimming pool.

As we drive toward the base of Diamond Head, the weather quickly changes. The clouds come in and set low over us. It begins to rain lightly as we start our hike up the volcanic mountain. The path gets slippery as we move up the hill and we warn the boys, to no avail. They run ahead and then back to us, laughing when they slip and fall. The rain feels good to me, too, tickling my skin. I feel alive and aware of every sensation around me. We pass a woman on her cell phone calling back home to tell them she is climbing Diamond Head. I look at Art and say, "She's missing it. She's missing the entire experience because she is too busy calling everyone to tell them about it."

We move on and the boys begin to feel the excitement of reaching the top. The weather still holds, light rain at times but never letting loose. There are few people on the trail and while many are wearing rain jackets, all four of us seem to welcome the moisture.

"Mom . . ." Rider says slowly, "Kathy, Shea, and Tanner

are here with us. Right now." My mouth drops. Art whispered the same feeling to me ten minutes ago. He said he was feeling them because of the anniversary.

"Really? How so?" I ask, trying to seem nonchalant.

"I can see them. They're right over there." He points up ahead on the trail. "Do you see them?"

"Not now." We walk on, holding hands. I close my eyes briefly. "I'll try to."

"When we get to the tunnel up ahead, I want us to dance. Let's dance for our angels." Rider, ever thoughtful and sensitive, is planning a celebration.

"Okay. Sounds good. What kind of dance?"

"I don't know." There is a pause, and I know he is thinking. Burke and Art are thirty feet ahead of us on the trail, and Rider wants to talk. "I haven't talked to them in a while. I haven't needed to. If I ever need them, they are there, just like that." He snaps his finger. It is so pure and normal to him.

"What do they say to you?"

"They come inside of my head. If I have a problem or question, they come to me with the answer. I just talk to them, and they answer."

"I love that, Rider," I say.

"When I'm mad at school and feeling like I can't do something, I ask them to come inside me and help me do it." He pauses to gauge my reaction. I smile to reassure him. "One day I was mad at Chase and I was going to yell at him. I saw them—there were three heads like a foot in each direction and there was a bubble around them. It was Kathy,

Shea, and Tanner. They stopped me and told me that Chase had had a hard morning and needed someone to be nice to him instead. He just didn't know how to ask anyone. So I was nice. It helped."

I am beyond words.

He runs ahead to catch his brother and father. It is his turn to be the leader of the hike. The rain abates and I reach up to slick back my hair. I think to myself about the purity of it all—the beauty of these two boys, for Art and myself; living our own life and yet remembering the ones who have died. There's a connectedness, a force that only strengthens in time, that guides each of us in our lives.

I revisit the bad dream, play it over in my mind. I try examining it logically and then something in me shifts and the pain and fear that's so authentic surfaces. Thoughts flood over me as if I am in a crowded room listening to hundreds of people talking. One voice is stronger so I tune the rest out and listen. "The dream was a gift, a sacrifice, given to make you more complete. You have always wanted to understand Art's pain, in order to be more compassionate with his loss. Seeing your own children close to death in the dream gave you that. You have now been in his shoes. You are blessed it wasn't real but now you understand the desperation, the horror of his experience." There is a pause, time for me to digest the words, then, "You have your own pain. Pain from losing Rod, pain from failures and insecurities. You have too much insecurity. You don't trust and you miss opportunities out of that fear. You must look into the face of the ugliness in life in order to see the beauty of it. Don't run from it, walk into it. You must be humbled in order to go deeper." Another pause. "This is the sign you have looked for and will understand later in life. The answers are within you. Keep seeking. The gift, my dear, is in the compassion—the compassion for Art and for you and for all of creation around. It was a dream, Allison. Your husband lived it. Maybe there's something in this for him as well."

I find myself walking next to Art and the boys, tears swimming in my eyes. I sit with the message. I look at Art as he plays with the boys. I think of what he has gone through. I still can't imagine.

I feel as if I am kneeling before life. I am humbled by it.

I tap Art on the shoulder and he looks back at me. I hold my hand up to my heart and rest it there while the tears fall onto my checks. The boys tug at his arms, daring him to race. He holds my gaze and puts his own hand to his heart and smiles. The boys see our body language, roll their eyes, but leave their mom and dad alone and walk ahead. Art reaches for my hand, entwines his fingers with mine, and we walk in silence for a while.

"I need to tell you more about the bad dream I had last night. It meant something and I want to share it with you," I say. We are almost toward the bottom of the volcano as I finish telling Art about the dream and the voices.

The rain has picked up again to a strong sprinkle. Art catches up to the boys just ahead. The few hikers left are wearing their raincoats, seeking protection. I leave my hood down and feel the heavy drops. I don't want protection. No more. I tilt my head back and welcome the pelting on my face and hair. My body feels alive, as if it had fallen asleep and is now waking up. I don't want to miss any of this.

Everything Is a Part of It

ONE EVENING A COUPLE OF YEARS AFTER THE HIKE ON DIA-
mond Head, Piper and I go out to dinner to celebrate her birthday. It's a ritual we perform every year, even though she is
married and has two young children of her own. Piper is my
firstborn child, and our connection is deep. Her daughter and
son are like sister and brother to Rider and Burke.

After an appetizer and a glass of wine, she reaches across
the table to take my hand and says, "Dad, there's something
I've always wanted to ask you. How did you survive that awful
time in your life? What made you keep going? Why are you
still a positive, loving person? Why do you still believe in the
goodness of life? Why didn't you choose a different course?"

"A different course? What would that have been?" I ask
her.

"Oh, Dad, you know, you could have killed yourself; you
could have shut down and gone away emotionally; you could
have lost yourself in anger and depression. There are a lot of

places you could have gone that might have been easier than the road you chose."

My daughter was my close companion during some of the darkest hours of my journey, and yet she still wants to hear these things from me. I sit quietly for a few minutes, gathering my thoughts, and then I begin to answer her.

"Piper, those are tough questions. Talking about what happened, to my family, to me, to the world around me, is one thing. But really understanding why and how I am here, and then trying to put it in words, I honestly don't know if I can.

"I've thought about these things from time to time. Deep inside me, there is a persistent sense of awe about it all. How do we survive terrible losses? I think each of us does it in our own way, calling on all of the strength and support and belief and faith that we have available to us. When I look back at my own story, I understand parts of it, and there are pieces that are still a mystery. I don't know that I'll ever be able to put my arms completely around them."

Piper responds, "I understand that, Dad. I doubt that you'll ever be able to say, 'Yeah, I see it now, here's how it all came to be.' But I still want you to try to explain it to me."

Daughters can be very persistent. I can see that I'm not going to dodge this one.

"All right then, Piper girl, here are some of the things that I believe about these questions.

"At the very beginning I knew only two things. Kathy, Tanner, and Shea were gone, and I longed for them in every part of me and during every moment of each day. That was a bleak, bleak time, and I had no basis for hope. What kept me going then? Piper, you had a lot to do with my staying around in those first days. You were at the foot of my bed when I turned off the lights at night, and you were there when the sun came up in the morning. You put aside everything that was important in your life to be with me. You were my only remaining child, and your love for me was so pure that you glowed with it. That love gave the first meaning to my life after the accident, and it carried me through the horror of those early days.

"The truth is, everything was a part of it. It seemed that everything in my world conspired to keep me afloat, to keep me moving forward, to support my belief in myself and the universe. Family, friends, and people I don't even know watched over me and took care of me, and as the years have gone by they have continued to do so. I have always felt a genuine kindness in other people, but when things go really wrong that kindness is intensified. We are linked to one another by invisible ties, in deep and primitive ways that we don't really understand.

"The other day I was wandering around barefoot in our backyard picking up dead branches blown down by the wind. A young gardener who was working in a neighboring yard shut down his mower and walked over to the fence to tell me that he often thought about me and that he was glad to see me doing well. I had never met the man before. That's how people have been. I have felt embraced and cared about wherever I went, even if only by the softness behind some stranger's eyes. These people wanted me to stay on this planet, they wanted me to heal and grow, they wanted me to be fully alive again. How could I possibly have quit in the face of that much love?

"And then, of course, there was Allison, and eventually Rider and Burke. I am still in wonder at how from the ashes of utter loss another family has grown. In some ways it is much like the family that I lost, and that is an unusual blessing. But in many ways my new family is unique and wonderful in ways that I could never have imagined, and that, too, is a great blessing. Above all things, they are the reason I am happy again and that my faith is strong. I love them fearlessly, and it is clear that we were meant to be together. The boundless love and support that we have received from the very beginning from Kathy, Tanner, and Shea are testaments to that, and Allison helped to complete my connection to them."

Piper interrupts my rambling monologue. "It was more than just people, though, wasn't it, Dad? I remember some of the conversations that we had about what you were feeling and experiencing. You said some pretty interesting things about what you were beginning to believe."

"I'm sure I did, Piper. I still think people were the most essential part of the healing process, at least for me. Maybe it was because they were the most tangible; we could touch each other. But from the very moment that rock struck there was some greater force at work. Three were taken, I was left behind. It has always seemed to me that there must have been a reason for that, maybe because blind fate is such a hopeless alternative. Their destiny was elsewhere, mine was here. Maybe I needed to learn something more, maybe I had something to give to others, I don't really know.

"In any case, I understood early on that I had a choice. I could stay the course and embrace life, or I could take some lesser path. Ultimately, there are really only two directions that we can choose—toward life or toward death. Since I felt like I had some sort of job to do, something not yet finished, the natural course was to keep going, to make the best of things. The moment I started down that road, with my head up and love in my aching heart, I knew that I had chosen well, and the blessings of the passing years have surely confirmed it."

Piper steps in again. "Dad, not too long after the accident, you told me that you felt like you had a lot to die for and a lot to live for. Do you remember that?"

"Yeah, I do. Once I understood that my family would always be with me and waiting for me, living this life to the fullest made even more sense. Ram Dass helped me with that."

Piper says, "Thank you, Dad. That feels really good to me. You know I'll never stop asking you questions like this. It's my way of checking in with you. It seems to me that in some ways your journey has just begun, and I'm always going to need to hear about how you're doing, about what it's like now."

Coming Home

WE WALK INTO THE ICE ARENA—RIDER, BURKE, ALLISON, and I—and I put the hockey bags down as the boys run to the glass to watch the game in progress. Hockey is a popular sport for boys—and increasingly for girls—in Colorado's mountain towns, and Rider and Burke have been skating and playing hockey since they were four years old.

"Dad, come look!" Burke calls out to me. "This is where we play next." It's a big arena, the ceiling of the dome darkening in its far reaches. The sheet of ice sparkles, shining white and alive. I close my eyes and listen to the echoing sounds—the scraping of blades against ice, pucks traveling from one stick to another, sticks whacking against other sticks and body pads, bodies caroming off boards, all in pursuit of the mighty puck. These sounds have become part of my own rhythms, part of being a father, and they are the sounds of before and of now.

"Where do we get dressed?" Rider wonders. I open my eyes but I can barely hear his words. I've gone back to another time, and I've lost my hold on the present. Allison looks at me, squeezes my hand, and says, "I'll take care of the boys." She picks up their bags and scoots them off to the locker room. Other parents and players are arriving, so I walk to a quiet section of the arena. I am alone, finally, with this rink, with myself, with the very center of me.

I look around, taking in every detail, reliving that day, that game. I haven't been back here, to this arena in Vail, since the day my life changed ten years ago. And once again, I'm here for a Mite hockey game. Then, it was Shea's game; now it is Rider and Burke's. The tension between past and present is almost painful, but there is also a strange beauty in the truth and oneness of it all. Ten years of sorrow and joy. The wild mix of emotions began on the drive over from Aspen this morning, and being in the arena has brought everything home. I realize now that I needed to come back to this place. It started here, back in 1995.

"Dad, look at Shea play. He's good." Tanner and I are in the stands together watching the game, a few other fathers nearby. "He's a natural." Tanner's pride in his brother is clear.

In spite of being more than four years apart in age, Tanner and Shea have been taking skating lessons together for some time. Tanner is smooth and fast on his skates, while Shea makes up in determination what he lacks in skill. Tanner has never wavered in his support of his brother. Shea has somehow fit into his life like a well-worn baseball glove, and Tanner has shared with him his sensitivity and depth of character.

Shea has always belonged wherever he was. It was his birthright to be fully alive in the now, and he has helped his brother to understand the look and feel of self-acceptance. The hockey rink is Shea's new arena in which to excel and to show the world what he is made of. He belongs here—it is evident in his natural aggressiveness, his desire to be wherever the puck is, and his zest to take it to the goal.

"Isn't this the best? Shea's been watching you play for years. Now it's his turn." I put my hand on Tanner's shoulder, proud that this young man is my son. He's growing up, his body changing all the time. I run my fingers through his long, light brown hair and give him a fatherly nudge as we watch the game. We smile at some of the less experienced kids wobbling around on their skates, giving it everything they've got. They may play on championship teams someday, but this is how it begins.

"He's gonna be good. He's made for hockey," Tanner says of Shea.

"Yeah, you may be right," I say.

One of the dads leans over and begins to ask Tanner questions about his own team, the Squirts, and who they play next. Tanner is a defenseman, and he loves the game with a passion.

"I'm going down to watch with Mom," he says, after talking to the father. "I'll be back up later." He takes the bleacher steps two at a time to the bottom, where Kathy is cheering on the Aspen team from behind the glass. Tanner wraps his arms around her neck and begins shouting as Shea gets hold of the puck. My whole family is down there, playing and watching, and I know how blessed I am.

Cheers and laughter erupt from our section as Shea

scores a goal—for the other team. Mite hockey is a beautiful thing. It is purity and innocence and second chances. Shea is cheering for himself, stick in the air, with no idea that he has scored at the wrong end. The coach is smiling and shaking his head. Kathy looks up at me with a big grin, then Tanner a second later, and we are all connected. We're a family—one that has had its struggles and pain but has persevered and come out the other side. I leave the other families that I've been talking to and go down to join Kathy and Tanner. Suddenly I want to be with them and closer to Shea on the ice.

Returning to this ice arena has caused time to collapse. Past and present are flowing around me, blending and separating to the point where I'm not sure I can distinguish between them. I'm afloat in a dream world of my own, and ten years ago and today are as one in my heart. In this time and place the joining of lives and loves is almost seamless, and I'm aware that I have long awaited this moment and that I may have been given a fleeting glimpse of the eternal connectedness of things.

I've struggled sometimes, though less now than in years past, with my love and devotion for a family that is gone, that died, and the deep and abiding love that I have for Rider and Burke and Allison. I used to wonder if one would diminish the other, if the new love would come to replace the old. And the truth, we have found, is that we are connected in so many ways that love has flourished for all.

From the beginning Allison has made birthday cakes to

celebrate Kathy, Tanner, and Shea's birthdays, and she still does. When the boys were able to walk and began carrying around pictures of Tanner and Shea, Allison told them that they were their special angels. When Rider or Burke is worried about something or having a tough time, they'll pray to their angels to help them through it. Rider even sees them sometimes, and he'll come and tell us about it, as he did on Diamond Head. As I write this, on the wall in front of me is a collage of pictures of them, inset with Mark Helprin's powerful words of memory and devotion, and I sometimes lose myself in their eyes, their smiles. And Kathy and Allison, of course, are in touch all the time, often in the middle of the night when Allison is trying to sleep and Kathy wants to talk. Kathy is part muse, part critic, part inspiration for Allison, and for some lovely and unknowable reason Allison has embraced her in it all. I have, too. They are still so much a part of me, of us, and they seem awfully close by. I don't know how or why this is, but it is so, and I suspect it has always been this way in our world. They have simply gone ahead into the light, to an unknowable place, and they touch us with their love and longing. We've had to reach for the connectedness, we've had to stretch our faith and our devotion to bring it alive, and it has made all the difference. We share a joy that has no bounds.

I slowly emerge from my trance and wander down to the locker room to join Rider and Burke while they are dressing. "Dad . . . over here." Rider wants help with his skates and some tape work on his stick. Kids are all over the room, in varying stages of readiness. Elbow and shoulder pads are flying around and sticks are in the air as parents do battle with their young boys to get them to concentrate long enough to finish the job.

Allison looks over at me, checking in. She is searching my eyes for clues, asking in her own intuitive way how I am, how my heart is, whether I need her. I pause while tying Rider's skates and smile over at her, letting her know that I'm fine, that a small piece of my universe has clicked into place.

I've always loved this ritual. Getting the equipment on, tying the skates, kids screaming and laughing, everyone having fun. I feel like a true dad when I'm doing these kinds of things with my boys. They are a rite of passage, one that I have enjoyed for a long time.

"Dad, are you going to watch our whole game?" Burke wants to know as I begin tightening his skates. I look up at him. He is so like Shea sometimes that it's hard to take in. "Yeah, my friend, every minute."

"Good. I'll score a goal for Shea." Now where did that come from? This child just keeps on touching my heart.

"I'd love that," I say, my eyes down as I finish with his skates.

As Allison and I stow away the boys' street clothes in their hockey bags, I hear our friend Jeanne come into the locker room with her twins, Jack and Willy, both of whom play on the Mites team. As I look up at her I remember that she was in Vail with us that day. Her older son, Tyler, played with Shea. She was here; she, too, bears witness to these memories, these connections. Jeanne smiles at me, reading my face, and comes over to give me a warm hug.

"Okay, guys, listen up." The coach is ready for the pep talk. I lean against the wall of the locker room, watching Rider and Burke and the other boys, feeling the moment. I'm here for another Mite hockey game, and I'm the happiest dad in the room.

Burke scores the goal he promised and after the game we decide to celebrate with ice cream. We walk from the arena into the center of Vail, to the same corner store where I took Kathy, Tanner, and Shea years ago. I decide not to say anything about it to Rider and Burke.

"Alf, this is it. This is the place." We're standing outside as the boys rough-house in the outdoor mall.

"Are you okay with this, Art?" I can tell she's a little freaked. "Are you sure this is where you want to go?"

"Yes. I'm sure." I turn around and smile at Burke and Rider beating up on each other. "Guys, let's go. It's ice cream time." They rush in, unaware of the footsteps they trace.

There were many times in the days following the accident that I wondered, what if we hadn't stopped for ice cream? What if we had taken ten more minutes getting it or left Vail five minutes earlier? What if I'd driven a little faster or a little slower? What if? I'm glad I let go of those unanswerable questions. That path leads only to madness.

We look over all the flavors. Allison is watching me out of the corner of her eye. Her protective cover is almost tangible.

"I want that one, Mom. What is it?" Rider asks.

"It's rainbow ice cream. Do you want to try it first?"

I stand watching, in stillness.

"No. It's what I want."

"Okay," she says. "Burke, how about you?"

"Hmmmm." He looks up and down the choices. He tries three kinds. He wants to have the perfect flavor. "I want chocolate."

Allison hands the cones to them and turns to me. I brush the moisture from my eyes as I order a chocolate sundae and pay the boy behind the counter. I wonder what he thinks about this grown man who is standing in his store, crying. We walk outside and wander slowly back toward the car, eating our ice cream.

"Hey, hon. You all right? Let's stop for a second."

"No, I'm okay." I look over at her, allowing the boys to move a safe distance ahead. "Those are the same flavors that Tanner and Shea ordered. The exact ones. And I had a chocolate sundae."

She watches the boys eating their ice cream and lets it sit inside her. She's comfortable with it, at peace with the mystery, and when she looks at me with a quiet smile I am more in love than ever. With all three of them. The coincidences seem without end, and we have come to welcome them and to know them for what they are, bridges in time, gifts from eternity.

As I drive west through the valley of the Eagle River I experience a vague sense of dread, aware that Glenwood Canyon is ahead. The boys are in the far back watching a movie, just as Tanner and Shea were doing on that day. In the rearview mirror their heads are resting together against the seat.

"What were you and Kathy talking about on the drive home?" Allison asks, putting the elephant on the table.

"Well, I know we talked a little about the hockey game and how much fun it had been to watch Shea, in his first away game. It's hard to remember the details, but we were listening to music before she drifted off to sleep." I think for a couple of minutes. "We also talked about the book she had just finished, the book signings she was doing. She was in a good place in her life. Her mom had died of cancer six months earlier and she had been present for it, she'd been able to say a peaceful good-bye. I think her life held a sense of security that she'd never had before—a completeness, maybe. I just remember how nice it was that she and I were happy together. It wasn't always that way."

"Dad?" It's Rider from the backseat.

"Yeah, buddy?" I say.

"I wish Burke and I could have known Tanner and Shea." I thought he was immersed in the movie. We purposefully had been talking softly. "I'd like them to be my real big brothers."

"Me, too, Rider man." Me, too.

"Well, I kinda feel bad saying this," Burke chimes in with his young voice, "but I'm sort of glad they died because if they hadn't we wouldn't have been born."

Hand it to Burke to be clean about it, to put all his cards on the table. Rider is giving him an incredulous look, afraid for my feelings.

"I can understand that, Burke. I think I'd feel that way, too, if I were you."

Some things are better left alone. I can't touch this one any further than that. It's hard enough to resolve in my own heart. Two families that I love with everything I have, that I couldn't choose between, not ever. I look back at them and say, "I love you guys with all my heart. Always."

We come to the place in the canyon where the accident occurred, and I pull over against the right-hand guardrail. In the summer after the accident I brought flowers here. Allison came with me. That time, as I was driving slowly along the right lane looking for the flattened barrier where the boulder had come through, a Colorado Department of Transportation employee pulled in behind me. I stopped, told him who I was, and asked if he knew the exact spot. He looked at me quietly, sadness in his eyes, and then said, "I'm very sorry for your loss. I was working that day here in the canyon and, well, I'm just so sorry." He had me follow him around the next curve, pointed to the site of the accident, and then backed his truck a hundred yards or so up the highway and parked along the right shoulder, yellow lights flashing, to allow me a few minutes free of traffic in that lane. Another kind man whose name I don't know. I placed the flowers on the wall of the canyon and looked up at the high cliffs where the boulder once rested and where the three globes of shimmering light had risen on my lost family's passage. I sang my silent song of longing and sadness, returned to the car, and drove on. Allison had asked me then what it was like to revisit the scene, what I was feeling. I remember telling her, "They're not here. This is not where their spirits live."

I walk across the highway now, lean on the rail, and look down at the river running fast and clear far below. The waters swirl around and over the boulders in the creek bed. One of them crushed our lives, senselessly, without intent, without meaning. For a brief time I am empty and alone, so much of me blindly swept away. And then I return to the car, to Allison, Rider, and Burke, and I am filled with my love for them, my joy in their very being. I have come, strangely, to a place of peace. I have come full circle, on a journey that I have found I cannot adequately describe. I am a man of greater faith than I have known, and I am not as afraid as I once was. I trust in the mystery of hope, I trust in myself, and I can touch others.

As I climb back into the car, Allison reaches across and holds my hand and I turn to the back to embrace the boys with my heart. We drive down out of the canyon, through the high shining mountains, into the rest of the day.

Upon Reflection

Grief Has No Rules

LIKE MY DAUGHTER, PIPER, MANY PEOPLE WHO KNOW OUR story—as well as those who hear it for the first time—try to imagine how Allison and I have dealt with the tragedies in our lives. We hope that what you have read so far answers many of these questions, but we thought we would set out some final thoughts that may be helpful to you when confronted by your own losses or the losses of those you know and love. We also share some ideas for people who want to reach out to a friend or neighbor when a tragedy happens. We don't pretend to have all the answers or even to know what is right or wrong in most situations. All we bring to the table are our own experiences with grief and loss. I lost a wife and two children, so I'll try to talk about that, while Allison will deal more with suicide and with another kind of loss that she did not write about in the story.

One of the truly beautiful things about human beings is how different we are from one another. We express joy, sadness, disappointment, failure, and success in our own individual ways. The manner in which we experience and express grief can be even more varied. Whether you are braving your own tragedy or simply want to reach out to someone else who is in emotional pain, the most important thing to remember is that grief has no rules. None whatsoever. Each of us approaches grief in our own way, and some of us do a better job than others. When tragedy strikes, all bets are off. The old ways won't work any longer, and the road ahead is unknowable, uncharted, and shrouded in mystery. It is a terrifying time, filled with fear, uncertainty, and a paralyzing longing for those who are gone. Our world will not be the same again, and we are forever changed. Who am I now? Only the shadows know, and it's time for me to begin finding out.

You ask, "Why should I bother, why should I endure this pain?" And you know the answer. "Because it is written that I should. I don't know where. It just is. It is not my time. My job is to stay the course, to bring meaning to this loss in the way I lead the rest of my life. To touch and help others, to teach those that come behind. And to love and protect the ones who are gone. This is a high calling, and now it is mine."

And so you ask, "How, then, do I do this? How do I survive, how do I move on, through and beyond this awful grief, this darkness?" And I learned the answer to that one, too. An hour at a time. A day at a time. Taking your eyes from the ground and looking a little higher each day until suddenly there is a glimpse of blue sky, of a star, and the world very gradually becomes brighter. Miłosz had it right in his poem "On Angels," and perhaps this is the only rule:

day draws near
another one
do what you can.

Support from Others

As I look out and back at what has taken place in my life since the boulder crashed down onto I-70, I understand better than I did the importance of the touch of other human beings and what we can do for each other when things go terribly wrong. People, and their abiding love, faith, and hope, are what carried me and helped heal me in the beginning and down through the years. Within myself I learned the indomitable power of the human spirit. For much of my life I was hardly aware of it. I know now that it resides in all of us, waiting to be called upon. Have no doubt that it is there, although with any fortune you will not have to reach for it often. And from others I learned the great power that an expression of caring, concern, and encouragement can have in helping someone in deep sorrow.

It helps, too, to live in a small town, or even a small section of a great city, where the residents' bond is so strong that they come together to carry and protect their own, whether they know them or not.

Personal grace and communication are key elements of the support system of someone who is grieving. In the beginning, some may want a lot of people around, while others need to have time alone to grieve privately. It is best not to project your own way of doing things onto someone who is grieving. Instead, ask what they want and need from you, and try to give them what they ask for. It is also important not to take anything personally during this time; emotions are high and raw, and the loss will be accompanied by a lot of fear and anger, which may be released on the ones we love most. If you are the one grieving, try to reach out to those with whom you feel safe. As counterintuitive as it may feel, this is the time when you need to let other people in—not all the time, but make room for the ones you trust most. Love and compassion and all the other good things that loved ones want to bring to you can't do their urgent work unless you allow them in. Open your broken heart to them, if only a little at a time. They have a miraculous desire, and power, to help that heart heal.

I also learned that a place of grief is a tempting place from which to judge others, particularly their motivations. It is true that they don't feel your loss the way you do. The fact is, they can't, so don't expect them to. Here again, my experience taught me to trust people's intentions, except where the evidence is strong that you can't. Probably the most difficult thing was not judging myself too harshly, and the only advice I have on that is simply to trust that you are doing the best you can, from moment to moment, from day to day. It happens to be true; it's just not easy to see. So as you work through the shock of your loss, try to let people know what you need from them, and try to let them give it to you. It will help them as much as it helps you.

In the first days after the accident what helped me the

most was to have people around who were close to me or to Kathy, Shea, and Tanner. Close friends took over the everyday details—organizing the food that people brought to the house, manning the phone and filtering out all but the few calls I really needed to respond to, and otherwise making sure that my visiting family members were comfortable. Unobtrusively but effectively, they also saw to it that I kept up my strength with food and drink. These friends acted as a buffer zone, and they helped to keep me at least marginally sane when the rest of my world had descended into chaos. As I look back I realize how important it was to me to have a few of these good people present throughout each day. I am normally quite happy when I'm by myself, but in those early days it would not have been good for me to be alone, and in truth I didn't want to be.

The support of a professional grief and loss counselor was also vital for me. It is not my nature to ask for help—a failing that many of us men seem to share—but as I descended into desperate grief and hopelessness, I had just enough sense to comprehend that I couldn't do it alone. At times I so completely lost my bearings that I felt as if I was going mad, and I was afraid I might not return. I sought out Brad Ham, who became my tether, my lifeline back to the light as I tumbled into the darkest recesses of my being. His strong hand was seemingly always there when I needed it most, and I grabbed that hand more times than I like to admit. The greater the loss, I think, the more important it is—and at the same time the more difficult it is—to face head on the emotions that are consuming you. Blindly twisting and falling down the rabbit hole of grief is a scary thing, and a trusted counselor can make all the difference. It is immensely helpful to know that you are not going crazy, that it is far better to stay in the pain than to run from it, and maybe above all that it will not kill you. As with everything else in the grieving process, counseling is an intensely personal matter. When you find the right counselor, you will have begun to create a *temenos*, a private sanctuary in which to experience the crazed and terrifying jumble of feelings assaulting you.

Time and Space

There are myriad books and poems that explore grief and loss in all their elements, and I encourage you to read widely in this literature. You will take from each what you need, what feels right to you, and leave the rest for someone else. Like counseling, reading about others' experiences of loss helps you to cope with the feeling that you are all alone in this, that no one else could possibly feel these feelings or think these thoughts. The words of others that have been there are comforting, if only while you are holding the book, and they can help you understand the various stages of the grieving process. Two books that I found particularly helpful were C. S. Lewis's *A Grief Observed*, which the author more famous for the Chronicles of Narnia and other books first published in 1961 after the death of his wife, and *Only Spring: On Mourning the Death of My Son*, by psychiatrist Gordon Livingston.

While most of these stages are undoubtedly essential, in my experience the greatest gift you can offer yourself (or someone else in sorrow) is the time and space to feel every feeling and to do all the things you need to do in your own journey of pain. I remember going through Tanner and Shea's drawers and closets and choosing which shirts and jackets and other items I was going to give away to charity and which few I was going to keep for myself. I have always been glad that I kept some of their things, and I'm even more thankful now that Rider and Burke have worn almost all of them. Touching things that belonged to them, that they wore against their skin, helps to bring them back to me, to keep them closer and clearer. Sometimes I would lie down on their beds and take in the smells of the pillows, the stuffed animals, hoping for some connection to them through their scents, their toys, their presence there. I could only do these things when it felt right to me, and sometimes it was months after the accident. With Kathy's personal belongings, I kept pieces of jewelry that I'd given to her or that particularly reminded me of her, and I let Piper and Kathy's closest friends go through her closet and drawers and jewelry boxes so they could choose the things that they wanted the most to keep. The rest of these belongings, too, I gave away so that someone else could enjoy them. While a couple of her closest friends have looked over her personal journals and other papers, I have kept these at the house, along with her photographs and slides. I think she would want that.

Grief not only has no rules, it has no borders and no time

limits. Death is so remorseless, so terribly permanent, and it requires the most difficult adjustments that a person will ever have to make. Each of us must face it in our own way and in our own time, and no one else can tell us how to do it. Grace with yourself is crucial—be patient with yourself, and above all wrap your arms around yourself and turn your love and compassion inward, where it is really needed. Reading about the experiences of others can be useful, but the essential direction comes from within. It is your journey, and yours alone, and you must take it in the way that works for you.

For me, the grieving process went on for years, although I would say that the most intense period was the first twelve months or so. Three birthdays, a year of holidays, those were hard times. Then, of course, there was the first anniversary of the accident, one of the most poignant days of my life. Yet when those milestones had passed, the way ahead was somehow clearer. I guess it's true that time can help heal the most terrible wounds and that the intensity of grief gradually softens as you adjust to living without those you have lost. I have a wonderful new family—and I am acutely aware of how blessed I am—yet to this day I miss Kathy and Shea and Tanner, I still long for them, and I am crying as I write these words.

Reaching Out to Others

There are so many kind and wonderful ways to reach out to someone who has suffered a tragic loss. If there were a magic word for guidance here, it would be *intention*. If at all possible before speaking or acting in a time of grief, look inside and be clear about your purpose, your motivation, and try to center your words and actions so that they are truly directed to helping the one in pain. Often what meant the most to me were simple, heartfelt comments like "I am so sorry" or "My heart is broken for you." Those words were for me, not for the person who spoke them, they were usually accompanied by a hug or a touch, and they comforted me more than I can describe. There are also unhelpful remarks, or intentions, that should be avoided if at all possible. I would stay away from knowing phrases like "It was God's will," and I would do my best not to compare pain or loss with a person who is in deep grief. At least for me, the emotions and feelings were so intensely personal and so all-consuming that it was not a time to hear about what someone else was going through or had experienced in the past.

Lots of people want to bring meals or flowers, and I think those are great ways to reach out as well. Best of all, though, at least in my experience, are letters and cards. They are no substitute for a personal appearance, but many people do both, and for some people writing a note is as close as they can bring themselves to come during a time of intense pain, especially if they do not know you well. People find the most beautiful things to say when they take a few minutes to write them down, things that they might not be comfortable saying face to face. There is something especially meaningful about a person taking time out of a busy life to write a thoughtful letter. It is an acutely personal action, and I believe that it is often appreciated far beyond what the writer could ever anticipate. I still have a basket

that holds all of the writings that I received from young kids
and friends and acquaintances and strangers—strangers are
the best, in their reaching out to someone badly wounded
whom they don't even know—and I look through them and
reread some of them from time to time. They take me back, but
now I welcome the feelings that they bring up, and even now I
am uplifted by the outpouring of love that the letters represent.
They were genuine acts of kindness, they touched my heart,
they made my imploded world a little larger, and they helped
me heal. Of course, I have a letter from a stranger to thank for
the serendipitous turn my life took. I am still in wonder that Allison took the time to write to someone she didn't know, and to
create a tape with so many of Kathy's favorite songs.

I have also come to understand that when one has experienced the loss of a child or spouse, there is an even greater
purpose in reaching out to another human being who is suf-
fering from a similar loss. Partly it is simply because I know
their pain better than most, and partly it is because I owe a
debt of gratitude to the many people who lifted me in their
arms that I can only repay by continuing the cycle of compassion. It is part of the deal, it seems, to be there for the next
guy, and the one after him. Those of us who have suffered great
losses, particularly sudden, inexplicable ones, have learned
things that came very hard, and if we can use that knowledge
to ease another's pain, perhaps to help the healing process,
then we have an obligation to try to make that difference. It is
part of our life now, part of the deal. I also find that it does
me at least as much good as it does the other person, al-

though I didn't know that at the beginning. Does it hurt to go into someone else's pain that is so much like your own? Yes, absolutely. Each time it takes me back to the moment when I lost Kathy, Shea, and Tanner, but it warms me to be with them again, even in those terrible circumstances, and I know that from that place of anguish I can best relate to and perhaps help in some small way the person I am trying to comfort. We have shared an experience of indescribable loss that not everyone can know, and in some deep place there is a connection, an understanding, that we will not find elsewhere.

Over the years I've met or talked with or written to a growing number of people who have lost loved ones. Most recently I spent a couple of hours sitting side by side on a busy outdoor stairway with a man who had lost his wife and soul mate of many years, and who was emotionally paralyzed in his pain. He told me wonderful stories about their love of traveling together, and I told him stories of Tanner's and Shea's antics, and I encouraged him to take up his travels again with some of the friends whom they had gone with in the past. We also talked about the need to try on new psychic clothes, new places and people, different activities, in order to paint life with some new colors to go along with the old. After the first few minutes we became completely oblivious to the flow of people around us on the staircase.

The meeting I remember most distinctly took place about a year ago in Denver, with a man whose wife and young children were killed by a drunk driver while walking across a downtown intersection. He, too, was present when they died, and he, too, was helpless to affect the outcome. I called him a few weeks after the tragedy occurred, and eventually I went over to his house in Denver to meet with him. It was awkward at first, as I don't think that either of us was sure why we were doing this. We gradually let our guards down, and he began showing me pictures of his family and sharing stories and memories of what they were like and things they had done together. I became more and more aware of how similar our losses were, mainly in the absolute voids that were left in our lives. He and I are very different men, but we had both lost everything that mattered to us, including all of our hopes and dreams. We had tears in our eyes as we talked through our experiences and our feelings and how we dealt with them. We asked each other some of the hard questions about the accidents and what took place afterward, questions that not many others would be comfortable with. We were strangers and yet we were brothers. Our shared grief connected us, and expressing that pain openly was good for both of us. I think of him often, and I send him silent prayers from time to time. We both know the other is there if we need him, but we know as well that we must make our own way. We move on in different ways, but we have a common goal—to keep our loved ones alive in every way that we can and to serve our worlds in ways that we hope will give meaning to their deaths.

Remembering

Probably nothing has been more important to my recovery process down the years than remembering my family. To this day Allison, Rider, Burke, and I celebrate Tanner's, Kathy's, and Shea's birthdays, we light candles and hold a short service of thanks for them at Christmas, we visit the gravesite together, we call them our "angels," and we speak of them as if we all know them well—which it seems we do. Their pictures are still all over the house, and I will often slow down for a moment and look at one of them, remembering. Allison has somehow caused these things to become a natural part of our lives, and I am deeply thankful for that. It has made life and death and life into more of a continuous pattern than the succession of abrupt beginnings and endings that it might otherwise be, and it has helped to keep Kathy, Tanner, and Shea very much alive for all of us and, to a degree, for those around us.

People are often reluctant to talk about those who are gone. They are unsure of what to say, and they are fearful of hurting the ones left behind. For myself, I have always wanted and needed to talk about them from time to time, preferably in a light and fun way. The memories of others have been an invaluable connection to my family, and I have cherished those memories whenever they have been shared with me. So if you've got some special remembrance of a deceased spouse or child or family member, don't hesitate to talk about it the next time you are with someone who loved them. If you're still not comfortable talking with a person who is grieving, write it all down in a letter and put it in the mail. Have no doubt—they will hold that letter to their heart.

You'll recall Mark Helprin's eloquent belief that love can

overcome death and that memory and devotion are what are needed above all to keep loved ones alive. Whenever you have the opportunity, do what you can to help people you care about honor and remain devoted to those who are gone from their lives, to keep faith. In my life there are a couple of other things that keep my family alive for me and within the community. Shortly after the accident I established the Daily Family Sportsmanship Award, which is given at the end of each hockey season to the player on each of our fifteen or so boys' and girls' Aspen Junior Hockey teams that best exemplify a short set of sportsmanship criteria. The coaches choose the recipients, and a big ceremony is held at a local ice rink to announce the winners and give out plaques. Any child can win the award—it doesn't necessarily go to the best athlete or the highest scorer—and for the hockey players in the program it has become an increasingly significant honor to win the award. The Aspen Junior Golf Association also named its year-end tournament after Tanner, and there are a number of young golfers in the valley with trophies from the Tanner Daily Junior Golf Tournament on their bookshelves. Friends also placed memorial benches at the elementary school and in a local park, and Kathy and Gaylord's book, *Aspen: The Quiet Years*, is still a popular seller at local bookstores. I mention these things mainly because they are illustrations of memory and devotion that are functioning and alive in my own life, they are part of the community in which I live, and each of them means a lot to me. Large or small, anything that promotes and protects the memory of someone who is gone is immensely precious and worthwhile.

Moving On

Life has a way of moving on with or without us, and I learned that it is a lot more useful, and satisfying, to get back on the bus at some point. I don't mean to suggest it is easy or even that it is free of doubt. Can we truly continue to honor and respect loved ones who are gone when we get back to our own lives? It is an inherent theme of our story, and I believe I have further emphasized in this afterpiece that the only way to truly accomplish these things is to create a life of fullness, service, love, and joy for ourselves and to take our loved ones with us on that journey. We cannot faithfully honor their lives, their sufferings and joys, their hopes and dreams, unless we live out our own to the fullest. Here again, there are limitless ways to go about this, and each of us must choose the course that works for us. My only real thought on the subject is, choose your own and remember that there are no rules in grief. Surviving great loss is a distinctly individual matter, and the lines will be drawn, inevitably, where life puts them.

With a new wife and two new children, I have definitely chosen to move on in a big way in my own life. Allison and Burke and Rider are my greatest joys, as were Kathy, Shea, and Tanner before they died. I feel incredibly blessed to have been given the chance to have another beautiful family, and in many ways the two families are one, but I had to deal with a lot of thoughts and fears about dishonoring my wife and sons who died. I met and became involved with Allison much sooner than I would ever have planned, had I been given the opportunity to plan it. I think that if Tanner and Shea had lived I might not have remarried at all or that it would have been years later in my life. Losing so much of myself in that brief moment in time left me so badly wounded and alone that I was literally ready to be reborn. I was probably as wide open and innocent as I had ever been in my adult life. I touch on this because I think many people wonder how long they should wait after they lose a spouse before dating or getting married again. I don't know of any bright-line conventions in religion or society that answer these questions, so it comes down to what each of us is comfortable with in all of the circumstances that are at play in our respective lives. Trust your instincts on this one. Ideally, I would have waited for a time for Allison to come into my life. It didn't happen that way, and I am forever grateful that we are together.

Love in Action

When I think about my own losses, what I felt, what I needed from myself and others and how I dealt with the grief, I have to be honest and say that I really didn't know anything in the first few days. Looking back, the one thing that I know I wanted—but didn't know how to ask for—was for someone to take over and take care of me. I wanted to curl into a ball and have someone protect me. I didn't want to be strong—which is my nature. And I didn't want to act like everything was going to be okay, either—which is in fact what I did, because I didn't know what else to do.

Besides losing Rod, I had two miscarriages after Art and I married. My love for Art, Kathy, Shea, and Tanner has helped me to understand loss a little bit better and helped me to believe that while we miss the person who has died very deeply and must grieve that loss fully, they can live on in our lives if we believe they can.

I had experiences—and still do—with Art's family that may seem "far out" to many. They were. They were certainly out of the ordinary to me at the time. I can analyze the relationship I have with them all I want, and I can doubt things that happen still, but what I know in my heart is that they came to me so that they could help their dad and husband. As a result—they probably knew this as well—they helped me and continue to help me. I can't explain it; I can only tell you that for me it is very real. I don't think it happens to everyone or that it should.

My belief, through them, is that when someone dies, they are very much there for the ones left behind. You may or may not feel them. When Rod died, I never felt him. I was too close to the pain. Even now, I have a hard time feeling his presence—but I know he is there.

I want to share some things that were helpful to me in my experiences with loss—both my own and those of friends who have experienced it as well. My hope is that if you have lost someone you will know, someplace in your heart, that they are there, watching over you and protecting you, and that what they want most of all is for you to eventually get to a place where you can feel joy again. They will never stop loving you and will always be there for you when you need them.

Support from Others

One of the hardest things for me to do is to ask for help from others. I am a very independent person and I want to be able to do it all on my own. When I lost Rod, I was twenty-three years old and too worried about my parents to figure out what I needed. Being strong can be a disadvantage if it causes a person to "stuff" the grief—which is what I did. When I began seeing a counselor, I found the one place where I could curl up into a ball and cry and be weak. Counseling was a big part of my healing there.

Years later, after meeting Art and doing a lot of crying with him, I realized just how important it is to let people in and let them be there for you. I did some more of my own healing over Rod as I cried with Art.

Grief can be a very long process, and while the strong emotions taper in time, to me the greatest gift a friend can give is checking in. Even now when ambulances go by, Art has a physical reaction to the sound and the knowing that someone is in trouble. It brings up the ride in the ambulance with Tanner. I reach out and hold his hand and let him know I care. I can't take the pain away but I can be a witness to his experience. It's what I needed with my missing of Rod, so I give it to others I know are hurting.

An incredible example of supporting others is the organization Valley Angels, a group that cooks meals, runs errands, and reaches out to help cancer patients in our valley. In volunteering with them I developed a close relationship with two people who knew they would be dying soon. In their last months, they talked to me about letting all else go except what really matters. Each had no qualms about letting others help them anymore because they realized that it was part of the giver's grief process as well as their own. Being in the presence of both of these women who had come to peace with their own death and watching them spend their final days loving and letting others love them was an incredibly humbling experience for me.

Grief support groups give some people a chance to realize they are not alone and in many cases they can share what they are feeling openly because everyone else in the group does understand. While neither Art nor I participated in organized support groups, I have met many people who have gone to them and have thought they were extremely helpful. For example, a girl I grew up with was killed in her college years by a drunk driver. Her mother started a group that was part of Mothers Against Drunk Driving and it has helped many other mothers whose children were killed the same way.

Liz, a friend, lost her husband in an avalanche, leaving their two teenage girls fatherless. I watched as mother and daughters let a community embrace them, reach out to them and help them to heal. According to Liz, in the first few months, after the service and after her extended family had gone home and she was alone, the most difficult thing for her was the phone. She would get so many phone calls every day that she stopped answering them (caller ID is a must, she said). It wasn't that she didn't care about the people calling or was afraid to talk to them, it was that every phone call meant an hour-long conversation and she simply didn't have the energy then.

She appreciated friends asking her to go on hikes, go to breakfast, or participate in other activities. It helped for her to get out of the house. Having friends to help with all the household and business matters was invaluable. Every single act of caring and compassion that came her way meant something to her and helped her to heal. The letters people wrote were very important and she loved the stories told about Jon. She loved hearing that people were praying and thinking of her.

When people reach out and touch someone who is in deep pain, they are making a difference. I remember Mother Teresa making a comment about how "we must put our love into action, for in loving others, we are loving God himself." To me, reaching out to others is one of the most valuable aspects of healing.

Time and Space

When Rider and Burke were four and five I got pregnant accidentally (I was on birth control but an antibiotic I was taking canceled the effects of the pill). Art didn't want any more children but I started getting excited. It was a difficult time in our marriage. When I showed up for the sonogram and the heart wasn't beating, I was devastated. My hormones were all over the place and I was a mess emotionally. Art agreed to try again. After getting pregnant right away, I miscarried again early in the pregnancy. I needed a lot of time and space in the beginning. I had a lot of anger and I had to process all the emotions and feelings by myself first. I remember my friend Andi trying to reach out and touch me and I totally pulled back. I just couldn't let people in for a few weeks while I dealt with it all myself and with Art.

The hard thing about miscarriages is that the hormones overtake a woman's body and magnify the loss of the unborn child. In my case, it affected my rational thinking. Though I miscarried early in both cases, I truly felt I had lost a child. This is hard to describe, but even from the beginning of a pregnancy emotionally you begin to imagine which sex it will be and to plan your new life with that child. For me, because I feel so horrible during a pregnancy (sick, low energy, food aversions), my body and emotions seem consumed and fixated on the fact that I am pregnant. In other words, I couldn't divert myself very easily, so instead I thought about it. A lot. After the pregnancy failed the second time and my emotions went wild, I found that the inner turmoil brought up a lot of my past pain from Rod's death and other aspects of my life. I was having a hard time letting others reach out to help me, which is a common symptom of depression.

Once again, for those reaching out to help and comfort, communication and grace are the key. I wanted to talk and to know that people cared, but sometimes the sadness took over and I couldn't let anyone in. Know that the person will come through it and each day usually gets a little better. Don't take things personally. Instead, respect the needs of the person grieving. If you are the spouse, just love her and hold her and listen when she is ready to talk.

Unhelpful (and Helpful) Comments

While logically I knew that a miscarriage could be God or nature's way of taking a child that might have defects, I might have yelled at someone if they had said that to me at the time. I also wasn't ready to hear "You can always try again." I was in a lot of pain for a few months, and that pain very often came out in the form of anger. Comments like those only hurt my feelings. The most important thing people could say to me was, "I heard you had a miscarriage and I want you to know how truly sorry I am for your loss." Or "I want you to know that I am thinking of you."

Friends who could just be with me and not judge the mood I was in were great. One friend would hike up Buttermilk Mountain with me a few times a week. When I first saw her after the second miscarriage she hugged me and said, "You know what? I have no idea what you are going through because I haven't had a miscarriage. My pregnancies were both fine. But I can tell you this, I know it must hurt deeply and so, for that, I am so sorry. Let's go hike. If you want to talk about it, you let me know. Otherwise, I'll bore you with my life." For a week or two I let her do most of the talking and I just allowed myself to totally focus on her. It reminded me of something Father Scott, a priest friend of mine, said many years before, "When you are in a lot of pain, one of the best ways to heal is to focus and reach out to help others. It keeps you out of self-pity."

The main advice I can give is to talk to people from your heart. When someone has lost a loved one, tell him or her you are sorry. As uncomfortable as it might make you feel to talk about these things because death is a scary topic, come out of your own shell and, as authentically as you can, love him or her in some small (or big) way, depending upon your relationship.

When Rod committed suicide one lady dared to say to someone else loud enough so that I could hear that his death must have been God's will. One of my good friends pulled me out of the room so I wouldn't react, but I cannot explain how hurtful that sentiment was. The friend who saved me from that situation is the same one who set up a massage (with a massage therapist she knew could handle my situation) for me a few weeks later. I cried through the whole massage and felt so blessed afterward. I have found that in my times of loss or pain I want to be touched but don't know how to ask. People who even just reach out and put their hand on my arm while they talk were helpful.

My friend Liz, who lost her husband, explained that the most unhelpful comments to her were when people told her what to expect, whether it be from her grieving process or from her future. She never tired, however, of people telling her she was in their thoughts and prayers.

Suicide

Suicide is a uniquely hard loss because of the particular brew of conflicting emotions it often brings to those left behind—sadness, anger, guilt. For me it brought out a lot of anger toward Rod; in fact, I had to work through the anger to get to my sadness over missing him. I was angry at him for leaving me, for hurting my parents and my brother, for giving up on life. My mother automatically took on the guilt of Rod's suicide. Mothers want to protect their children and think that they have raised them to feel good about themselves—loved and nurtured and wanted in this world. When a child commits suicide, all of what a parent thought he was giving—or was supposed to give—goes into failure mode. It didn't matter how many times I told my mother that it wasn't her fault, a part of her psyche always has felt a sense of responsibility for his leaving. It's probably her own way of holding on to some part of him. She has always wondered, "What if I had . . . ?" There are a thousand ways to fill in that blank from the time the victim is born, and suicide only exacerbates it. This is true whether the person who commits suicide has been diagnosed as mentally ill or not.

Once again, what meant the most to our family were the people who showed up and cared for us. People who had lost a child were very helpful to my parents. The community in Austin brought food and flowers and showered us with love. People who came to be with us, to sit and be a witness to our devastation, meant the most.

I think many marriages are challenged greatly when there is the loss of a child. I watched how hard it was on my parents. My mother had her own way of grieving and my dad had a totally different way. I can only express the importance of not judging others while you go through your own process. Take your own path and try as hard as you can to let others go on their own path. We are all so different; men and women especially handle emotions like grief differently.

When a Child Dies

The death of a child is unlike any other death. It leaves parents and siblings alone in their grief. Each parent is trying to deal with his or her own pain and they are also trying to help their other children deal with theirs. It is a very hard time for a family on many different levels. Each family member is facing the death in their own way and realizing what that loss means to them. Resentments can form easily if it doesn't fit in with the other family members.

When Rod committed suicide my mom and I openly expressed our pain and loss by crying and sharing with each other and friends. My brother and dad internalized their grief, as I think many men tend to do. They chose to work through it on their own and not openly talk about it. It didn't mean they weren't grieving. They had never learned how to talk about that kind of pain and I'm sure each was afraid to talk about it because he thought it would send my mother and me into tears. All four of us had a hard time communicating our needs because the pain was in the way.

I have seen many families who have lost a child become hardened. Each person in the family has built their own wall of protection around their heart that enables them to function in the world around. The problem is that in most cases that leads to loneliness and isolation.

When I met Art I learned the value of honest, open grieving. I think one of the reasons he has been able to move on in such a healthy way is because he allowed all of his pain to surface and come out of him. He didn't have other family members to take care of so he cried and cried and looked at every aspect of the pain and his life without his family. He still does.

Just recently Rider played two hockey games in Vail. The team and the families went to eat pizza after the first game. Burke, Rider, Art, and I walked over to the small pizza joint with the others. We walked in and I looked at Art and tears were brewing in his eyes. He said, "Allison, this is the pizza place where we ate . . . before we had ice cream . . . and had the accident." I froze. He just sat there and felt it and wasn't ashamed of his emotions.

Everyone has different emotional capacities. I am one of those people who enjoys feeling every emotion and isn't afraid to explore them. Art is very different in his everyday life—as are my dad and brother. I don't think there is a right or wrong way. I think we are just all different. I do encourage each person, in the face of death, to feel as much as you can and to know that with help from others you can come through the pain and into a space where you can remember and honor and continue to love your lost child with every piece of your soul. You can still be an alive, happy person who, while completely missing your child that is gone, holds true to yourself and that child.

Healing, I believe, does take feeling all of the emotions. Just remember that you must take care of your own journey in the grief and not judge anyone else's. Just because your mate, for example, is not showing all that they feel does not mean that they are not feeling as much as you are. Try not to judge. Rather, love. I think that if you try as much as you can to love and make that effort in honor of your child, you are giving them the greatest gift of all, even though they are gone.

The Bright Light in Grief

As Art wisely put it, "Grief has no rules." I couldn't agree more. The way I handled it was different from Art, from my mom, from my dad, from my friends who have suffered losses. It's personal and painful and each of us has our own journey through the grieving process. The bright light that I see shining through is the ability for other people—friends, family, community—to touch your life and to help make you strong enough to heal. We have the capacity to heal and grow when really bad things happen. We also have the ability to reach out and love others—and through that loving, I think, we gain the most.

For Kathy, Shea, and Tanner

Acknowledgments

This book began because our angels wanted it written. There is no other explanation. Allison would wake up in the middle of the night and not be able to go back to sleep because she knew she was supposed to write something down. She would go to the computer and type it out, pecking away with her index fingers at amazing speed. Usually it was a recounting of something from my life with Kathy, Shea, and Tanner, as scenes and events were shown to her. She would e-mail her writing off to me at the office at 3:00 a.m. or whenever she was finished, and I would read it the next morning. The accuracy of these narratives was often startling.

For years we had been discussing my writing a book about loss and recovery, mainly to help others in the midst of great losses of their own. The practice of law, two young boys, a wife I wanted to spend time with, and an admitted reluctance to set out on the arduous path of telling a coherent personal story combined to keep me from it. Allison's writing began to encourage me to move forward. When we were in Hawaii and Allison had her terrifying dream of losing our own boys, she began praying for guidance about where to go with our dream of writing a book. The message she received—get in touch with Pam Houston and Mark Helprin, two of our favorite authors, and ask for their help—prompted Allison to write them both. Remarkably, they both responded with inexplicable generosity.

Pam as much as anyone probably deserves the credit for getting me to put my first words on the page. She stopped in Aspen on one of her travels to meet this girl who had been e-mailing her out of the blue, and we ended up having one of the more memorable dinners of my life. Pam listened to the story and told me to write it, that it needed to be told, and that it would make a difference. I asked her where I should start it, and she told me "at the beginning." The following Saturday morning I went down to the office for what would be the first of countless weekend mornings in front of the screen, and I wrote the initial pages of this book under the simple heading of "The Story." Oddly, I began to enjoy the process of feeling my way back into the events of that time, sometimes dissolved in tears with the memories, sometimes glowing with joy from those same memories.

And Pam continued to be there when we needed her, particularly with the organizing of what seemed to us to be a complicated tale. We weren't sure if it should be only my account, or if it was to be from both of us, how to create that. Allison's midnight rambles were producing a lot of words on a wide variety of subjects, and Pam helped her to improve and focus her writing style. She guided me in getting my emotions down on the page. Facts I understand; feelings are tougher to get your arms around. We all agreed that the story had to be told in two voices, and that is what we set about creating. The three of us became great friends, sharing our stories and lives as together we weaved the book. There's a country song that goes something like, "She's got a playground sense of justice / she won't take odds / . . . I think everything she touches / Turns to gold." That's Pam Houston all over. We love you, girl, and we are forever grateful for your firm touch.

Mark Helprin, too, became a kindhearted and thoughtful correspondent with us, and he provided us with much needed advice about the publishing business. It is in his writing, though, that I have found the wildest inspiration. Mark knows that the human spirit is unquenchable and that it lives in the furthest reaches of our imagination.

Sarah Flynn is a writer's editor. She took our manuscript and helped make it a book. She did every sort of editing possible and in the process gave us her heart and became our friend. She worked fluently with our two voices, and she often seemed to understand what we wanted to say better than we did. It wasn't easy for me to turn the story over to her, but I developed a deep trust in her skills, her instincts, and her intentions. How did we find her, among the hundreds of editors that appear on the PublishersMarketplace website? Here again, Kathy sat on Allison's shoulder as she studied the list, and Sarah's name basically jumped off the page. When Allison called her, Sarah cautioned that this might not be her kind of book, but she agreed to read it. She loved the story, and a wonderful relationship began. Since that first call, she's been with us every step of the way, and we owe her beyond gratitude.

Sarah introduced us to our incredible agent, Michael Carlisle of Inkwell Management. He, too, believed in our story, and I don't know that anyone else could have worked the miracles that he did in getting us into the hands of Harmony Books at Random House. As an agent he's part prince, part magician, and all professional. He not only cared about our book, but he also put his heart on the line for us. He's our mentor and our friend.

Harmony Books is an amazing combination of revered publishing house tradition, professional skills, and personal touch. The moment we walked in and met Shaye, Julia, and the rest of the team, we knew we'd found a home. Publisher Shaye Areheart had a unique vision of what our book could be, and the whole tough-minded bunch of them let us know from the outset how much they believed in the potential for our story to touch the lives of others. Julia Pastore's editing has been sensitive and insightful, and the book you've just read is far better for her contribution. She has organized the moving parts of publishing a book in wonderful ways. We were told not to expect it in the publishing world, but at Harmony Books, everyone on the team—including Julia's assis-

Acknowledgments

tant, Anne Berry, directors of publicity Annsley Rosner and Campbell Wharton, and marketing manager Kira Walton—has been a joy and an honor to work with.

Thanks to our publicist, Meryl Moss. She believed in us and this book, and for that, and all of her hard work, we are very thankful.

Thank you to Lacey French and Mike Campbell of Visual Intent, who designed our website.

My daughter, Piper, has always been here with me. She lived this story, and she has been involved in the writing of it as well. She's my only girl child, and she's been the finest blessing.

I know I've spoken about it before, but I want to acknowledge once again the people of our small town. They carried me in the dark hours, they encouraged me when Allison came into my life, and they have helped our boys become capable young men. The people of Aspen have given me humility and love and grace. That's what a village does.

Finally, Allison's brother, Doug, has been a constant encouragement to us in the writing of this book, and her mom and dad have reviewed our many versions and have been our cheerleaders. Thanks also to my brothers, John and Mike, for their love and support.

Rider and Burke spent a lot of mornings with a sleepy mother and a lot of weekend days without their dad, who was at the office writing. They've known all along what we were doing, and they've continued to tell us how happy they were that we were doing it. They made the greatest sacrifice of all. They have been very much in our hearts as we wrote this book. Early on I read them some of the tougher chapters. Now they have the whole story.

About the Authors

Art Daily is a partner in the Aspen office of Holland and Hart LLP, the largest law firm in the Rocky Mountain West. He specializes in real estate law and represents many well-established clients in the Aspen area. He received his B.A. from New York University and is a graduate of the University of Colorado School of Law, where he was editor in chief of the *Law Review*.

Allison Daily graduated from the University of Texas at Austin with a business degree. She is the codirector of Pathfinders Valley Angels, a nonprofit organization that serves Aspen-area cancer patients undergoing chemotherapy. She works as a substitute teacher in the Aspen public school system and as a unit clerk and bereavement counselor in the obstetrics department of Aspen Valley Hospital.

Visit their website at OutoftheCanyon.com.